T0062926

Twelve Hours

by
Irene Coombe

Order this book online at www.trafford.com
or email orders@trafford.com

Most Trafford titles are also available at major online book retailers.

Print information available on the last page.

ISBN: 978-1-4120-5517-8 (sc)
ISBN: 978-1-4122-3475-7 (e)

Trafford rev. 01/04/2022

 www.trafford.com

North America & international
toll-free: 844-688-6899 (USA & Canada)
fax: 812 355 4082

Acknowledgements

I would like to acknowledge the great love and support given to me freely by these friends below:

Pat McBride, Sandi Hill, Jim Slack and colleagues at Strathclyde Police and Los Angeles Police Dept. Joanne Wilson (and her church for their healing prayers), Myra & Clair Mc Kendrick, Jackie, Susan and Diane who must have sore ears by now.

The Sally's (You know who you all are).

The staff at Specsavers Clydebank especially Mr. Kinsey.

All the staff at both Yorkhill Hospital for Sick Children and The Southern General Hospital Glasgow. Especially Dr M Donaldson and Mr. R Hyde.
&
More recently
The Pituitary Foundation.

Dedicated to the loving memory of my late parents:

Mr & Mrs William F. & Ellen Mc. B. P. Small

{Willie & Ellen}

Eternal love & thanks

To my husband Stephen, son's Sam and Stephen
and
daughter Kirsty.

also

To my wee brother
for the support (ha, ha).

Twelve Hours

1

Monday 1 February 1999.

I will never forget this day. I hope that somewhere, somehow, someone is having the greatest day of his or her life, because we are having our worst.

Tears sting and blind me. The noise of my son's screams is deafening: "Mummy, please help me, it hurts, they are hurting me mummy, tell them to stop, please mummy, help me, help me..."

My heart breaks.

Will these be his final words?

Stephen's sparkling blue eyes glaze over with tears. His pupils are dilated by fear, and the ferocity of his struggle has caused the tiny capillaries in the whites of his eyes to burst, forming a tracery of blood-red threads. Under his pallid skin, the veins in his neck bulge into taut blue ropes.

His speech is mumbled now. My little one is looking up at me as though he is deep under water, tears streaming down his face. He seems unable to reach the surface and breathe – breathe *life* – and I am the one holding him firmly down. I feel that I am drowning my own sweet boy.

Inside I scream, but I will not let my son face this trauma alone. No matter what it takes I will be by his side. I will not give up hope, not even as I burn up inside. I will stand by him as if my own life depended on it.

It takes four people so far – two female nurses, one male, and myself – to keep my little baby still so that the anaesthetist can get him to sleep.

Will this sleep last forever?

I am nauseated by the heady, pungent smell in the room, sticking thickly to the back of my throat. The bright whitish fluorescent lights dazzle me, and my eyes begin to twitch. I feel strangely irritated by the clip-clopping of the staff's mules on the cold lino floor. I look momentarily at my own footwear – fluffy pink slippers with teddy bears on the top, a Christmas gift from my daughter for my stay in hospital with Stephen. No one had realised they would soon be splattered with her little brother's blood.

We are in the pre-theatre room, about ten feet square and superheated by an array of lights. I can see sweaty circles in the armpits of the medical staff's tops. The nurses, doctors, anaesthetists and myself are all sardined around the high metal operating table, with my precious child in the centre. There is hardly enough room to swing a cat, never mind try to comfort my dying child.

I try to concentrate only on Stephen, keeping all my thoughts with him. For a moment, though, I must look to the ceiling to dam my tears in my overflowing eyes. I do not want to let Stephen see me weeping and know that I am as scared as he is.

The grimy creamish walls are scuffed and scratched by equipment trolleys, and marked with bits of bluetak and cellotape. Cupboards and shelves containing medical supplies extend to the ceiling: plastic tubs with all sizes and colours of needles, small bags of cotton wool balls, a variety of rolls of sticking plaster. But the scariest things are in metal trays. I hope against hope that the doctors don't have to use these alien instruments while Stephen is awake. For my part, I never imagined I would be in this situation, confronting all this fear-provoking equipment for myself.

In the corner to my right are two dilapidated canisters

containing the anaesthetic gas they will use to put my son to sleep. Even on our way along the corridor to this room, I was enveloped by its distinctive stink. As soon as the lift doors opened it made my stomach churn.

Opposite the door we entered is the exit that leads to the operating theatre. The room is designed this way in case of an emergency. I pray this will not happen today, not with my baby. I hope, too, there will be no call for the ominous three level metal trolleys on the other side of the room marked **RESUCITATION.**

All of us wear theatre gear to help prevent infection. Over my shoes I have thin white paper slip-ons with elasticised tops, and on my head is what looks like a white paper shower cap. The nurses and doctors have also donned surgical gloves, but at least I have not had to wear them. I can stroke Stephen's soft baby skin to comfort him, wipe away his tears and touch his little chest, its heart pounding under all this stress. I wear a pale blue paper gown over my own clothes, the same style as the cotton gowns the staff wear. Underneath, I have on my lucky purple shirt, the one I was wearing when I won £7000 the previous year. Then, excitement and wonder were my feelings. Today, by contrast, I am gripped by fear – the fear of losing my own precious child.

I worry now, that Stephen is frightened by the surgical mask obscuring my face. I lean over his tiny body and kiss his little chest. He is so warm and sweaty. I kiss his red cheeks and forehead.

This is such a strange world I am in here today. Like all parents, I had never even contemplated that any of my children would be so ill as to need major surgery, let alone brain surgery. I steel myself. I must help the doctors and nurses or my little boy – "ma wane" – will die.

Stephen must have surgery today because there is no time left. The cerebrospinal fluid is building up in ventricles around his brain, distorting it into a cone shape. This condition, hydrocephalus, is very dangerous. The tumour on his pituitary gland – the cause of the fluid on the brain – must be removed as soon as possible.

Please hurry, get him to sleep and end this hellish living nightmare. I just cannot hold on much longer. I am confused and hurt. Why am I letting these people hurt my baby? Why does everything have to be so difficult for us?

My older children, Samuel, aged 15, and Kirsty, 12, are with my parents today. I don't know what to say or how to explain to them what the procedure will be, or even how long it will take, and I cannot tell them what the outcome will be because neither the doctors nor I know. I want to reassure them that their little brother will be OK, but I don't know how to, and I want to hold and comfort them but I cannot be in two places at once.

How must they be feeling?

It is their little brother who is ill and they want their mum to comfort them. I also want someone to hold *me* and comfort *me* and tell me everything will be all right. But there is no one. My children's dad, my husband for 18 years, just a few weeks ago walked out. My children and I have been left to scale this enormous mountain alone.

It has been over half an hour now, the longest half-hour in my life. The medical staff are having great difficulty getting Stephen anaesthetised. All the nurses, the anaesthetist, the consultant, the medical students and I are pinning Stephen down onto the cold hard operating table, to no avail. I am virtually lying on top of him to keep him still, as the staff hold his legs to prevent him frantically kicking out. Meanwhile, the consultant grips Stephen's arm in an attempt to cannulate him. My little boy struggles again and again to grasp the gas mask and tear it away from his tiny face.

I can feel the build up of emotion inside me. I scream silently. I long to tell them to let go of my baby. Stephen is so small and precious; although he is seven years of age, the tumour has affected the growth centre in the brain so that he is the size of a four year old. But today he has the strength and determination of a giant.

I am trying desperately to calm him, and I will promise him anything at this moment. Over and over again, I gently whisper:

"The doctor is going to take all the bad soldiers out of your head, the ones that hurt your head so much and make you so sick, then the doctor is going to put in your head lots and lots of good brave soldiers to make you all better. You'll see, soon you will be able to go out and play with all your friends again in the park, and we will have a special holiday together."

"Come on son, be brave for mummy. Mummy is here with you and when you wake up mummy will still be here with a big, big surprise for you. Sam, Kirsty and mummy love you very, very much, and we will all be here to see you when you wake up."

These are the last words Stephen hears from me today.

Will they be the last words he ever hears?

Though I present a calm facade to Stephen, conflicting thoughts swim in my head.

Should I hold him down and help get him to surgery, the surgery that might save him, or should I release my precious baby, tell them to stop, and cuddle him tenderly as he dies without pain in my arms?

With a heavy heart I banish these uncertainties from my mind. I must give Stephen the best chance of survival.

2

During what might have been our last Christmas together, Stephen saw the TV commercials advertising a large red toy car. He was very excited, and wrote to Santa Claus to ask for one. I told him then that it is the well-behaved children who get a visit from Santa. I will make sure he gets one now.

I intended to make this an especially memorable and happy Christmas; this was, after all, the first one we were spending together without the kids' dad. I took the kids to the Glasgow town centre to see the Christmas lights, which are famous for their originality and beauty. The illuminated display is complemented by the most beautiful nativity scene. Looking into the glass case at baby Jesus with Mary and Joseph, I felt very abandoned and alone.

Why, when I needed my husband to be so strong and supportive at this difficult time, was he not?

I was reminded, too, of the meaning of this celebration, the fact that it is not all about gift-giving but rather the gift of life itself. If I only had known what lay before us, I would have spent more time at the nativity scene in quiet contemplation.

Glasgow's George Square at Christmas is turned into a huge outdoor ice rink, with a refreshment tent at the side. As you walk round the square, delicious smells waft from stalls selling candy, hot dogs, popcorn and mulled wine. There are rides, too, for the kids, included a twisting chute, a circus wheel and a beautiful carousel. Another stall sells everything that you could imagine that twinkles: hats, wands, gloves, tiaras, crowns and baby bibs.

Over recent years we have made many journeys to this fun place, and always take lots of photos. I treasure them, even more so now as I realise this could have been our last Christmastime with Stephen.

That night, we stood huddled in minus ten degrees watching Kirsty and Sam ice skate.

We are decked out in festive touches: Stephen, Kirsty and Sam's hats light up, and mine plays music. Having lost a great amount of weight since my husband left, my winter jacket hangs loose on me. Stephen is cold despite his many layers of clothing, so I unzip my jacket and snuggle him close to me. I can smell the sweet sweat at the back of his neck. There we stand, my baby and I, tightly bound together, happily watching Sam and Kirsty wobble on the ice.

What fun we had – our sides hurt with laughter, our jaws hurt with smiling and our throats were raw from shouting encouragement to the skating siblings.

Keeping my promise, I have already bought a car for Stephen and I will give it to him as soon as I see him after his tremendous marathon of a surgery. I tell myself that I *know* he will wake up after his operation because he has wanted this big red car for so long.

I keep the thought of his lovely sweet surprised face in my head.

We have by now watched the kids on the ice for over an hour. We had to go and get a hot drink before we froze. Together, we all set off for Da Vinci's Italian restaurant, not far from the centre of town. Visits to Da Vinci's were a tradition for our family and I was not going to stop it now.

As we walked down the street, we window-shopped at all the boutiques. Passing a retro clothing store, we had a great laugh at all the unusual tops, jackets, trousers, hats and bags. Other passers-by stared at our merriment. We didn't care.

Nearer to the restaurant we could see the beautiful

blue and gold Christmas tree on display, with its array of baubles, tinsel, stars and chocolate figurines, the latter of which the restaurant staff gave to children who had eaten up all their food. A blast of heat hit us smack in the face as we opened the door. The walls were decorated with tinsel and multicoloured lights, and the friendly staff wore a selection of decorative hats, all adding to the delightful ambience. At last our noses, frozen by the winter cold in the town centre, began to defrost, and the aroma of garlic, pizza, sausage, macaroni and mulled wine was so welcoming that we could feel our stomachs begin to rumble.

I ordered four mugs of piping hot chocolate. It came in tall glasses decorated with various snowy scenes – each of us could pick the scene we favoured – and with delicious melted marshmallows on top. We drank deeply of the warming fluid.

This evening lives in my mind as one of life's precious moments.

3

I am putting all my concentration into keeping
Stephen as still and as calm as possible. I can only just
hear what the medicos are saying to each other, and I
know they are trying to keep their voices down. They
are muttering about how difficult this is, how they
have never had such trouble getting a child to sleep
before.

"Poor little chap," one nurse whispers.

"Poor mother, I would not like to be in her shoes
today," replies another.

They have to move quickly now. Stephen's body is
suffering because he does not produce the hormone
cortisone, which is necessary in times of stress and
anxiety and is normally produced in vast amounts
under these conditions. It is vital that Stephen gets a
large dose now. His lack of endogenous cortisone puts

his life in danger even before they start to operate.

However, there is a problem. He is running out of useful veins via which the medication could be injected; the more they try to put a needle in, the more the veins collapse, one by one.

"Try his foot," the doctor yells.

"No good," the anaesthetist grunts.

"Try his groin then," replies the doctor.

"Wait, I'll try the other foot first. No, this is no good, we are not getting anywhere and this little boy is beginning to slip away. I will have to put an arterial line into his wrist."

This is a very painful place to have a needle put, but now there is no other option.

"We are in at last," announces the doctor.

The line is finally in place, and Stephen is screaming blue murder. The sound from my little one is unbearable. His tear-stained face, his pleading eyes, beg me to help him.

"Mummy, mummy, help me, it hurts mummy," he cries.

I have to look away from his piercing eyes for a moment to collect some strength. The doctor has pumped in cortisone and other medicines, and the anaesthetic, thankfully, is now starting to work. Stephen is beginning to relax. The thrashing diminishes and he is now whimpering, gently drifting off to sleep. There are tears still running down his little cheeks, which are ruby red with the fighting he has put up. All this courage from a precious boy so small. He sighs softly and gently nods off, unaware now of all that is going on around him. His tender little heart is slowing down, its beat softening to a calmer pace.

I lean over his tiny, still body again, and kiss his hot cheeks, sweaty forehead and tiny button nose over and over, whispering a little prayer in his ear.

"Be strong, my baby, and please come back to mummy. I love you so much and I am so sorry you have to go through this."

I wish I was on that cold horrible table instead of my baby.

"I love you."

I close my eyes. Images and smells of his torment scar my thoughts: the horrid smell of the gas, the look on my baby's face, the intense struggle he put up, his tiny heart beating against his ribcage like a captive bird, his thrashing around in uncontrollable terror, the noise of the clanking metal trays and the cold touch of the operating table. These impressions will never leave me.

I say a silent prayer.

"Please God, help us today, guide the surgeon's strong and gifted hands. I know there are hundreds of thousands of people praying at this moment for themselves, but I ask you, today, please give us guidance and help my baby. And please, let Stephen forget this day!"

4

The sun had broken through the morning clouds and the sky was a bright glorious shade of blue. I could feel the sun's heat through the window, despite the early hour. Somehow, I knew that everything had to be all right on such a lovely summer's day.

At 5.58am, Thursday 15 August 1991, I was in the final stage of labour. I needed to decide on a girl's name before the baby was born, and I didn't have long to go. If the baby was a boy, I knew he would be called Stephen.

The clock alarm rang at 6am, with a funny intermittent sound because its batteries had run down. It seemed to me to be a sign. If the baby was a girl, I would call her Dawn.

At 6.08am a healthy 8lb 12oz baby is born. It is a boy. Stephen has arrived safely in my arms.

This had been a very difficult pregnancy with a few scares along the way. It is my third and last child because my body cannot cope with another pregnancy. The obstetrician had told me that as my blood Rh group is different from my children's and husband's, my body would destroy any other growing babe in the womb as if it were a foreign object. My pelvis had also split in the middle while I was carrying Stephen. This extremely painful condition made carrying another baby impossible, and would cause me to miscarry at an early stage. Still, we were very happy and did not complain. We now had three healthy beautiful children: a boy, a girl, and finally our littlest boy.

Life had indeed been kind to us.

As a baby, Stephen was every new mother's dream come true, a textbook infant. He would eat and then sleep for four hours every four hours. He remained contented through to toddler stage when, at the age of three and a half, he started his first mother and toddler group. We used to go over the road to the church hall on a Monday and Wednesday to meet up with all the other kids, their parents, and occasionally their grandparents, and we had a great time.

However a few months later, at the age of four, Stephen became quite withdrawn and quiet and would not mix with the other children in nursery school. I was a bit uneasy about this, as we were a very close and happy family and did many social things together and with others: picnics, zoo visits, seaside holidays and so on. My older two children hadn't had any problems with socialisation at nursery school.

Why was Stephen so different from my other children?

We persevered for a while hoping that school next term would be better as, by then, he would have gotten to know the children who would be in his class.

During the holidays, Stephen had his fifth birthday. We all had a fantastic day. We had hired a bouncy castle and invited all his nursery classmates. All our family gathered too – grandparents, cousins, aunts, uncles, nieces, nephews – as well as neighbours and friends.

Everyone loved Stephen. With his blonde hair, smiling face and pleasant nature he was hard not to love. The garden was full of laughter and giggling and sometimes a few tears as wee ones fell from the bouncy castle and bumped into each other. There were sweets, crisps, lollipops and a big magic birthday cake.

We had hired a clown named Mark for the day's entertainment. He got all the kids to sit in a circle on the lawn and showed them lots of tricks. He also blew up balloons into different animal shapes and colours for each child. He was quite a hit.

As the day progressed and the temperature rose, Stephen began to get very tired and sleepy. Unfortunately, as he was wont to do during that period, he was so exhausted that he went to bed and missed half of the day's fun.

We were quite used to Stephen going to bed during the day by then. Even when we would go to visit family or friends, Stephen would disappear only to be found in someone's bed fast asleep when we were due to leave. It didn't really bother me too much. But the other mums were saying that this was not right – a boy his age should have as much energy as the other children – and I should go to the doctors to see about it. I said I would, but put it to the back of my mind.

I was too busy! I was sending my last, my youngest baby, off to school. Stephen started the day after his birthday party. He joined the same line that his older brother and sister had at the same school gate when they were five years old. I had kept the school blazer I bought my first son in 1986 when he started school, and my daughter had worn it in 1991 when she began. Now Stephen was wearing it in 1996. I was so proud of my children.

Primary one went very well for Stephen; he did great work for his class teacher and was always the best-behaved child in class. I suppose this was because he lacked the energy to misbehave.

It was in primary two that there were some signs that something was not right with Stephen's health. The teacher had started to write notes home to me, expressing concern about Stephen's bedtime. She was worried he was not getting enough sleep, and had assumed that this was the cause of him nodding off during class.

I told her this was not so, and wrote to her on many occasions to confirm this. I explained that at home we had a regular routine for bath and bedtime and it had always worked for my other children. I couldn't understand why Stephen was so tired. Ultimately, I agreed I would see the health visitor about this.

The visitor explained that children were individuals and required different amounts of sleep, different amounts of food and different amounts of stimulation. I was to try some small changes in his diet, cut out some fast foods, try a variation of the bedtime routine, and see if this helped.

It didn't.

We struggled on for a few months. The best solution we came up with was to let Stephen have a sleep when he came home from school.

By the end of primary two in June 1997, he would sleep from when he came home from school until the evening meal. I would have to wake him for his dinner, bath him then let him go back to bed. Strangely, I didn't realise how much he was sleeping as I was too busy helping my other kids with their homework and getting on with the chores. Since both my husband and I worked fulltime, we were always preoccupied, running around and getting everything organised for the next day.

I had stopped noticing Stephen's absence.

5

As we organised a fundraising event on a lovely
Saturday morning in May 1998, my husband
announced, out of the blue, that he was leaving. The
kids' daddy admitted all the trouble with Stephen and
coming home to a busy and noisy house every day was
too much of a strain for him. He sought solitude
elsewhere.

On top of Stephen's troubling behaviour, we now had
to deal with my husband's absence. We didn't see very
much of him at all for over the next year and a half.
When I would call to tell him of a terrible episode
Stephen had had with his headaches, which were
worryingly frequent by this time, he would accuse me
of trying to get his attention by using the kids as
pawns. Of course, as would prove to be tragically the
case, this was not so, but I couldn't get through to him.
He was on a runaway train apparently enjoying his
freedom, and he didn't want to be disturbed by

anyone, especially me. So my children and I were left to embark on a long and terrifying journey alone, though I was at pains not to let anyone think I couldn't manage solo.

The summer holiday break from school had just started and I had arranged childcare with my parents. They would now look after the kids while I was at fulltime work. My parents, to my gratitude, tried hard to give the kids a good time, and arranged many trips and outings for them to parks, beaches, museums and even fancy restaurants sometimes. The kids, of course, loved being showered with affection and spoiled terribly.

One day, as I drove home from work, I could see my parents waiting anxiously at the garden gate for me. I was quite alarmed until I heard my mum squeak with laugher. As I opened the car door she said, "Come quick and see what Stephen is doing."

Entering the garden, I saw to my surprise and delight that my parents had bought the kids a large trampoline.

"Wait," my mum giggled, "Stephen, show your mum what you can do."

Stephen hopped onto the trampoline and proceeded to perform an Irish dance Michael Flatly-style. Mum and dad were just about rolling around the garden in fits of laughter, holding their sides. Stephen's face, however, was very serious; he was giving an Oscar winning performance. To us, at least, he was.

By later on in the holiday break, mum and dad had spent many long hours with the kids. One day, my mother took me to one side and told me that Stephen was always falling asleep and saying his head hurt.

"Do you know about this?," she asked. "Are you going to take him to see my doctor?"

Now I was beginning to get a bit worried: I had always trusted my parents' skills and opinions. I made an appointment with the GP.

We had to wait a week. When we finally saw the GP he asked many questions, such as whether Stephen had a rash, a temperature, any bowel complaints, pain, or anything else I had noticed that was out of the ordinary. I answered that he hadn't, apart from his chronic sleepiness and sometimes a headache.

The GP gave him a quick check over and could not find anything amiss. He concluded that Stephen was misbehaving and attention seeking, probably because his dad had gone. In his opinion children didn't really know what pain was. He told me that if Stephen had a "pain" again I was to give him some paracetamol and send him to bed. He then ushered us from his consulting room.

I went back to that GP on more than six occasions in that year alone, always with the same complaint about Stephen's headaches, and I was always given the same advice. I began to doubt my own opinion.

It was now late summer of 1998 and Stephen's headaches were becoming more regular – about eight weeks apart – and lasting longer, roughly two to three days. I would deal with his excruciating pain by giving him pain relief tablets, and holding a very cold cloth that I was now keeping in a plastic bag in the freezer to his forehead as I nursed him tenderly to sleep in my bed. I think his sleep came more from exhaustion than anything else.

As the weeks went by Stephen began projectile vomiting during the headaches. This would last for about half an hour or so, and once the vomiting and pain subsided he would sleep for hours on my bed in the dark under my pillow.

Although Stephen was complaining now about a very sore head, and that this was making him sick, the GP did not seem to be bothered. He was of the same old opinion – that Stephen was attention seeking. Eventually, after more than a year of complaining about these symptoms, I asked the GP to refer me for another opinion.

He abruptly replied, "I suppose you are not going to be

satisfied until I do refer Stephen to a paediatrician, are you?"

I sat there in amazement.

How dare he speak to me like this.

I had been very patient, had faithfully tried all the remedies he had suggested, and this was how he spoke to us.

In any case, I finally got the referral. We had a six-month wait for the specialist's appointment.

By now it was autumn. Stephen was in primary three, aged seven, and these awful headaches were ruling our lives. He was absent from school more often than he was attending, and the pain was forcing him to bang his head on the wall and scream uncontrollably. I was watching my baby in agony, but unable to comfort him.

What kind of useless mother was I?

I didn't know what to do. I had tried all the treatments that the doctors, other parents and friends had suggested but nothing was helping, nothing was relieving Stephen's excruciating pain. It had gotten to the point that I knew when Stephen's next headache would be, and I would organise my shifts at work so that I was able to be with him and nurse him on these days.

It was very exhausting for me, and difficult to watch. Also, I hardly had any time left for my other poor kids. With one child so ill, working fulltime, and being both mum and dad, my life was at breaking point.

On a number of occasions, the school called me at work to say Stephen was very unwell, and asked me to come and take him home. I did go to school and pick him up, but I had to go back to my work. I was in charge of the office and I couldn't leave a junior alone, as there was a great deal of money to be banked daily. I would gather bubble packaging from the stock room, put my warm winter jacket on top of it and make a simple bed for Stephen on the floor under the table in the office. This makeshift bed was more suitable for a dog than a sick child, but I did not have any choice. I was a single parent and could not afford to lose my job. Even so, if any of the senior staff knew I had Stephen there I would have been sacked immediately.

Between June 1998 and December 1998 we saw more doctors than we thought was possible for one person. I had also taken Stephen on four or five occasions to the accident and emergency department at the children's hospital. The registrar and junior doctor had not been able to detect any problems, and all Stephen's neurological tests were fine. Nevertheless, they referred Stephen to a paediatric migraine clinic.

In the meantime, we awaited the appointment with the paediatrician set for Monday 14 December 1998.

A few weeks before that date, Stephen's class teacher asked me to come and visit her urgently in the school. Stephen was not getting any of his class work correct, and everything he copied down from the blackboard was wrong. She asked that I take him to visit the optician and get his eyes checked.

Although I had had just about enough of Stephens's problems, I took her advice and made an appointment with my local opticians, Mr. Charles Kinsey at Specavers.

On our first visit it was immediately obvious that Mr Kinsey was a caring man. He smiled and gently lifted Stephen up to the examining chair.

"You are easy to lift, Stephen," he said. "Sometimes I need to lift big children to reach my chair and that puffs me out."

As he sat Stephen down he chatted for a while about football and fishing. I guess this was to put Stephen at ease. Then Mr. Kinsey started the process to ascertain Stephen's problem.

He asked Stephen to cover his right eye and say out loud what letters he could read. To our shock, Stephen said he could not see anything at all from his left eye. I looked up to make sure he had his eye open; he did. Mr. Kinsey then asked Stephen to cover his left eye and do the same again. There was very little difference.

It was apparent immediately to Mr. Kinsey that Stephen was blind in his left eye and had very poor vision in his right. He asked me if Stephen had any other medical problems. I told him Stephen had been suffering from severe headaches for some years now and that the doctors at the children's hospital had referred him to a migraine clinic. I didn't know if there was any link between the headaches and Stephen's sight loss.

Unbeknown to me, Mr. Kinsey was now on a long path to find out the reason for Stephen's eye problems. He told Stephen he had a little boy of his own the same age, and reassured Stephen and I that he would not stop checking and measuring everything until he had an answer.

I asked Mr. Kinsey what he thought was wrong. As he looked at me, he gently replied:

There can be many reasons why a child can lose sight, and sometimes it is temporary. I will do as many tests as I can, do some homework and if I need to I will refer you back to your GP."

"Don't worry Mrs. Coombe," he said, "we will find an

answer."

Mr. Kinsey's manner was so kind, measured and reassuring that he did not alarm me at all. Yet, after my unsatisfactory experience with our uninterested GP, I couldn't help but wonder what good a referral back to him would do.

Nevertheless I lived in hope.

First up, Mr. Kinsey would do a series of visual field tests, and we were to come back to his office the following day for them.

I went home and reflected on all this sudden urgency. Over the past years no one had been much interested in Stephen's headaches, and now the optician, a person I didn't think had any medical knowledge, was taking these symptoms very seriously. I called my husband to explain what was happening but, as usual, he didn't seem too bothered.

Over the next two days we went to the optician in the afternoons and Stephen completed the many tests. When the optical results had been established, Mr. Kinsey wrote them up and gave me a letter to take to my GP. I opened it on the way out, but I could not understand the information it contained: it was all medical jargon with eye measurements. All I could make out were the capitals in red ink saying THIS CHILD MUST BE DIAGNOSED IMMEDIATELY.

I delivered this letter personally late in the afternoon of 11 December to the GP's office, and went home hoping that Monday would bring us better news from the paediatrician.

Little did I know at the time that Mr. Kinsey, his wife, also an optician, and his father In law, an eye surgeon, spent many, many hours at home trying to find out the cause of Stephen's sight problems.

Mr. Kinsey had gone above and beyond the call of duty, and to this effort I believe I owe Stephen's life.

6

Monday 14 December 1998.

This was a day I will never forget.

It all started out so normally. Stephen was at primary school along with his sister Kirsty, Sam was in high school, and I was at work. Stephen was not due to endure his next headache for another ten days.

I was trying to think of a way of sneaking out of work undetected to take Stephen to visit the paediatrician. As the day wore on I began to think, also, of how was I going to manage to make Christmas fun on my feeble pay packet. If I only knew what was ahead of me, money would have been the last thing on my mind.

I had had so much time off work with Stephen being ill, I might have lost my job if I asked for more. I even seriously considered not taking him to see the paediatrician at all, as all the medical people we had seen so far thought there was nothing wrong with him. Perhaps I would just be wasting my time and putting my job on the line for nothing. Thankfully, after lunchtime I decided to have one final shot and attend the appointment. After all, this doctor specialised in children's disorders and maybe she could cast some light on Stephen's headaches. I collected Stephen early from school and we made our way to the clinic.

On arrival, a nurse took Stephen's weight and height asked a few general questions. She then told us that the paediatrician would be in to see us when she had finished with her current patient.

A few minutes later Dr Kate McKay, a tall slender lady with short dark brown hair and a sharp but concerned manner reminiscent of Jamie Lee Curtis, called us into her office. Smiling, she introduced herself and began the consultation.

"What has been going on with this young man?"

I recalled for her the terrible pain of Stephen's fierce headaches, the projectile vomiting, his long sleeps and the comforts I tried to provide for him, such as letting him go to my bed and lie in the dark with me cooling his brow with a flannel. I also told her I had noticed that he was still the same shoe size and clothes size as when he started school over two years ago. He had begun school the tallest in his class but now he was the smallest, and I had always assumed he would have a growth spurt and catch up.

At the end of our consultation and as a passing thought I mentioned that Stephen was having great problems with his sight, and that we had gone to an optician who had noted that Stephen was blind in his left eye and had limited vision in his right. I told her that the optician had written a letter to our GP.

Dr McKay excused herself and left the room, anxiously explaining that she was going to call the doctor's surgery and find out what the letter from the optician contained.

About 15 minutes later she returned. With a burst through the door that almost smashed it against the wall, she rushed over to Stephen and me and asked me to repeat this story. Looking at me intently, she listened to my every word as I recalled Stephen's litany of problems.

The look on her face was now one of great concern.

Putting her hand on my knee, she quietly said, "Mrs. Coombe, you do not seem to be the kind of person who panics easily. Therefore I am going to explain to you what I think is going on within Stephen's head. You have just described to me the symptoms of a brain tumour. I want you both to come to the children's hospital tomorrow where we shall do a CT scan to confirm. Are you alright?"

I sat back upright in the chair and thought to myself how silly this was. She was making a grave mistake, but I didn't think I should tell her. I decided to wait until they did the CT scan, so they would find out for themselves.

At home I called my parents and my husband to relay what Dr McKay had said. My parents came to my house at once to offer me solace. Then I had the task of telling Sam and Kirsty that their little brother was ill.

Two hours later my husband came to my house. I don't know if he believed me or not as he didn't speak to me. He just went into Stephen's bedroom and spoke to him. After about half and hour he gave Sam and Kirsty a pound coin each, and then left. He had not said a word to my parents or me while he was there.

The next morning the doorbell rang. It was a local florist with a beautiful bouquet from my workmates. They had included the most moving card containing words of support and comfort. This was when I realised things were serious.

We went to the hospital at 9am the following day and were greeted by a large contingent of doctors and nurses. They were all so very kind to Stephen as they took us into a room full of toys. The nurse asked me if

I would like some tea or juice, and offered Stephen juice too. This was so different from the shabby treatment we had received from our GP.

A neurologist, Mr. Stevenson, came in to see us next. He explained the procedure for the CT scan and reassured Stephen that it would not hurt at all; in fact, he said, it is like getting your photo taken, only this is a picture of the inside of your head. A nurse then came to tell Stephen that they would need to take a blood sample from him, and that she had brought along some magic cream to put on his arm so that he didn't feel anything. Stephen was very excited at this and offered his arm eagerly.

A few minutes later we were asked to follow another nurse to the scan room. The scan machine was covered with pop posters, cartoon pictures, and multicoloured baubles, and the table Stephen would lie on had a cartoon cover on it. The whole room was very warm and welcoming for children, but, just by virtue of the fact that we were there, was not so comforting for me. Things were made worse by my having to face this on my own. Although my husband was at my side he had not spoken to me at all day.

The nurses and technicians laid Stephen down gently and secured his head in a brace to help prevent him moving around and ruining the pictures. They put thick black straps over his head and another over his tummy with his arms tucked in. Stephen was not so happy about this but I was able to reassure him. He and I have a very close bond, and whenever I told him that everything would be alright, he would do whatever was required for me.

This bond in time was taken to its very limits.

The scan only took few minutes. Afterwards we had to wait while the doctors assessed the pictures in case they needed to repeat the procedure. Before we left the scan room I looked over at the window separating the control room from the scanner. I saw the doctors and radiography staff examining Stephen's film.

There seemed to be quite a buzz going on.

I knew I was right, there is no tumour in Stephen's brain and they are all trying to find one. They must be very embarrassed and dreading coming out to tell me.

I sat with a smirk on my face as Dr Stevenson and a nurse come back into the waiting room. The nurse asked Stephen if he would like to go with her, meet some more cute young nurses and eat some of their delicious Christmas chocolates. Stephen jumped up and almost ran from the room, not even bothering to say cheerio to me.

I know this is when the doctors will admit their huge blunder.

Mr. Stevenson starts by expressing his commiserations. He then breaks the news: "Stephen has an enormous tumour in his brain beside his pituitary gland, an extremely rare kind called a craniopharyngioma. I am unable to help him with this. I have a colleague, a neurosurgeon called Mr. Rab Hyde, and I know he has seen this type of tumour before. My secretary is calling him at this moment in London where he is at a conference. When I speak to him and tell him what we have found he will return at once. Do you have any questions?"

My world shattered. How wrong I was: not only did Stephen have a brain tumour it had to be an extremely rare one and, as I was to find out, in the most difficult place to access surgically.

Mr. Stevenson asked when Stephen is due his next headache, pulling me momentarily out of my shock. I told him we expected it in about ten days.

He then gave me the news I was dreading: "We would need to be in theatre before then. Stephen has hydrocephalus, fluid around his brain, and his brain is being squashed into a cone shape, which is what has caused the pain for so long. If we do not get the pressure released immediately, Stephen will die before his next headache. Do you understand your son is in grave danger and is very ill?"

I was stunned, and remained silent. I didn't know what to think or say.

My husband was with me, not that his presence provided any comfort. He sat there in his own selfish world, showing no consideration for my feelings. It would have been less worrying for me if he were not there.

I was aware Mr. Stevenson was looking at both of us. It must have been very clear to him that there were marital problems. I bet he was wondering why my husband was not showing me any warmth. He had not been there during the last months when Stephen was ill, and he was still no good to me now. I could feel the tension emanating from him. I knew he blamed me for Stephen being ill.

I sat with my arms folded, trying desperately not to show any emotion. I was so scared that Mr. Stevenson would ask if I was OK. I didn't know how to react; all I was thinking was that if this goes wrong, and is as dangerous as he says, my baby might die. In fact he said my baby probably *would* die without surgery. In my mind's eye I had a hellish vision of me looking into a little white coffin containing my last-born son.

No, No, No, it just can't be.

I have been going on and on at all medicos for years and have been repeatedly told that there was nothing wrong with Stephen except attention seeking or maybe migraine, and all this time my baby has had a time bomb in his head that no one could see.

Why?

If I had not taken the risk of loosing my job and attended the optician, my son would be dead within ten days. Today is December 15.

Anger, disbelief, shock, and grief overwhelm me.

7

Now, as I wait for my child to be anaesthetised, I think about how a little boy of seven should be at school, running, jumping, skipping, and playing games with friends, not lying on a rigid operating table with a sharp, shiny steel knife cutting into his precious little head as if he were a sacrifice.

I have an image of the brutal surgery that is soon to come: the surgical team will be using a power drill – a real power tool – to secure fittings and screws. It will be screeching, and it will give off a burning smell as it cuts through his skull, smoke rising. As they enter his brain with their instruments they will be trying not to damage his soft, delicate tissue, but it may be unavoidable. This, I realise, is the point of no return.

We have been holding Stephen down on this huge operating table, the one he hardly covers half of, for over half an hour now. Sheets and pillows lie scattered on the floor by the struggle. Bloody needles, tubes, wipes, surgical gloves and cotton balls are strewn about in metal kidney trays, remnants of the Herculean task of cannulating Stephen. He had been struggling so much, kicking his bare little legs and writhing all over, that, although he is weakened and defenceless, he had managed to detach the mouthpiece of the anaesthetic gas tube. The horrid smell of the gas had filled the room as panicked staff, lacking the time to repair the mask, held the tube against his mouth.

Now the gas has done its work and my baby is sleeping. I can slowly release my death grip on my little boy, my little brave soldier, my seven-year-old baby in the tiny body of a child of four.

As I am finally able to stand upright I notice that my back aches and my legs are numb. The lights in the room are dazzling, almost blinding me. One light in the corner has been flickering on and off, a fact I hadn't registered until now as I had been concentrating every ounce of my being on my baby. My heart is pounding so hard that I feel it is about to burst out of my chest.

My world is now closing in on me. I know I must still be alive, but try as I might I cannot get any air into my lungs. I gasp for a breath as wave after wave of terror sweeps through me. I try standing taller, sucking harder, leaning slightly backwards but my lungs are unable to expand and the pit of my stomach is unable to relax. The room spins. I feel that I am a volcano about to erupt. My emotions are white-hot molten lava, but whether the eruption will come from my head, my heart or my stomach, I do not know. I am sure the turmoil inside me must show on my pale anxious face, contorted now with grief.

I dread the imminent moment when my son will be wrenched from my arms.

I am no more than a bystander looking on, now, as all the medical staff go into autopilot. I stand there in everyone's way as they push past me to the left and right, not bothering to excuse themselves. A short time ago the staff relied on me to calm Stephen and help hold him down, his soft skin pressing against mine and his hot breath flowing down my cheek. I am not needed now. I am merely an extra body in a small room.

Their priority is Stephen.

I can make no more contribution now to saving my son's life. I, the one who carried him for nine months, the one who gave him the gift of life, the one who nursed, cared for, bathed, played with, taught and comforted him, am no longer required.

A nurse looks over Stephen's tiny body to me and cold-heartedly tells me to give Stephen a kiss. Without a trace of empathy for my situation she turns me around and escorts me to the exit doors of this fearful room.

I look up at the sign above the door.

Is this the "exit forever" door? Will I ever see my little boy again?

As we go through the door the nurse turns to me. She says, "This is a long and dangerous operation. We will notify the ward if we need to get in touch with you in an emergency. If you don't hear anything from us ask the ward staff to call down after ten hours. We should have an idea of what is what by then. Goodbye."

Is that it?

My mouth parched, my body aching, my heart thumping, it hits me that I have handed my baby over to strangers. He is out of my sight and out of my hands now. I do not know them.

Will they care for him the way I do?

Stephen now faces the biggest challenge of his young life and I have had no choice but to leave him to do this on his own.

What kind of a mother am I?

I exit the old, stained and chipped wooden double

doors into a busy and bright corridor. I am on my own now and I don't know where to turn. I need a loved one, a friend, someone to hold me, someone to reassure me. No one is here. I stand alone, drained of all emotion, but with one question playing over and over in my mind.

Why Stephen? In all this vastness, why Stephen?

I pray that God will guide the surgeon.

I have no idea what to do.

Should I leave the hospital and go for a walk on this beautiful bright February morning, or should I be quiet and still? Should I talk to people, and if so, what would I say? Am I letting my son down if I eat or drink? Why am I suddenly so calm?

The immensity of the day overcomes me. My feet take steps to I don't know where.

8

I find myself in my son's small room at the end of the ward. The room is very hot because it is February and the heating is on at full power. The windows are sealed shut: you don't want to have a child who has just had life-saving brain surgery fall from a fourth floor window. That would not make for a good recommendation.

Stephen has brought his favourite photograph of his little tan and white puppy, Taz, whom he loves very much. The photo sits by his bedside along with his favourite football team shirt and get-well cards from his gran, granda, big sister, big brother, family, and friends as well as a great big humorous one from his classmates. All the children in his class and the staff at his school have signed it. They wish him a speedy recovery, and say how much they will miss him until he gets back.

*But will he ever get back? Will he be back in this bed
or in my arms ever again?*

I look dry-eyed at the small hollow in the pillow where
his head had been. I have soothed, stroked and kissed
that little head for so long. A few hairs had fallen out
during the night as he was tossing and turning in his
sleep. I remember with delight the jokes and stories
we read together before he nodded off to sleep. This
sweet reminiscence gives way immediately to a cold
and vulnerable fear. Stephen's belongings are now just
objects in this impersonal room.

I picture what the surgeon is doing now to save my
little boy. I know he will slice open his scalp from ear
to ear, pull it over his face and bring it down to the
level of his eyes. He will drill out a large piece of skull
and put this into a tray to be replaced later. He will go
deep inside the complex folds of his brain, and
carefully remove what he can of this horrendous
tumour. When he has finished he will fix screws and
glue to hold his skull back in place, use metal staples
to hold his scalp together, and then bind his head
tightly in a large white bandage.

Will he ever look the same again?

Time has stopped for me. I think of my other children
and wish I had let them be with me now. But I was
trying to protect them from this terrible situation,

especially after what they have gone through with their father leaving us. They are with my parents today, and I know my mum and dad will take great care of them.

Over the last few weeks, I have been consoling my parents, family and friends telling them everything is going to be all right. Stephen is being operated on by the best neurosurgeon in this field.

Am I kidding myself?

The last conversation I had with Mr. Hyde before surgery was not so positive. In fact, I think most of what he was saying was not registering. He spoke softly to me, explaining what his plans were and what the outcome of this kind of invasive surgery might be. As he spoke the ward sister sat by my side, empathy emanating from her. I know she must have heard this many times before, but she nevertheless held my hand and comforted me as I needed it.

The blinds in the room were closed, but the winter's afternoon sunset was blazing through the gaps. I was wondering why were these gaps not fixed, then I remembered this is a NHS trust hospital: with all the cutbacks, blinds were probably last on the list for repairing. I remember squinting, trying to fix my gaze on the surgeon, attempting to appear to comprehend what he was saying, all the time wishing he would hurry the consultation because I needed to get out of the way of the blinding sun. It didn't occur to me to ask to go to another room because I did not want to appear ungrateful.

The surgeon began, "Ten years ago things were very different and we would not have gone to surgery on a child with this size of tumour and this amount of damage to the brain."

He told me that the medical profession was not so adept a decade ago at treating endocrine conditions such as Stephen's. They knew surgery could remove most of the dangerous tumour, but lacked expertise in panhypopituitarism, the deficiency of pituitary hormones which Stephen suffers as a result of his tumour.

I think to myself, thank God it is Stephen who has the tumour. Stephen at least has a chance, albeit a slim one, whereas if this condition had befallen my first boy, born over ten years ago, they could not have done anything to save him.

The surgeon continued, telling me that this type of tumour is extremely rare, affecting around one in five million, usually children. The tumour can be cystic, consisting of a bag of fluid around the pituitary gland that can be surgically drained. Although this is a risky procedure, it is less so than a craniotomy, the procedure that Stephen must have.

Stephen's growth is calcified and the size of a tennis ball. The hard tumour mass is compressing his brain, causing his terrible headaches. This kind of mass has to be removed manually by the surgeon, and the steadiness of his hands is paramount. Mr. Hyde explains to me that it is like attempting to pick pieces of chewing gum from soft cooked pasta without breaking any of it.

The surgeon concludes with these chilling words: "I am operating in the centre bottom of the brain and I do not think Stephen will survive. His chances of survival are 3%. If Stephen does live he will be severely mentally and physically disabled and blind."

Momentarily I am in a daydream state, a defence against the unimaginable terror I now face. I quickly snap myself back to reality.

In the corridor people walk past me, talking and laughing. Children run and skip.

Don't they know what I have just done! I have given my permission to let a man, a man I don't know, a surgeon, slice open my little boy's head from ear to ear.

Shouldn't I be crying or screaming or running up and down the corridor? Should I stop these people and tell them to be quiet? Don't they realise how strange I feel? Will it be their turn next? Maybe then they would not be so jolly.

I need someone to come and get me, to take me to Stephen so that I can cuddle him and kiss his sore head.

After three hours, a nurse quickly passes Stephen's room. She does not come in to see me, so I assume the operation is going well.

The corridor outside the room is long. It is painted bright colours, one wall yellow with big blue dots, another lime green with smiley faces on it. Even the nurses' station is funky with its fluffy orange and purple tassels. The ceiling has many mobiles hanging from it; I suppose this is for the children who are lying down all the time. The children who have had their surgery get a special turban bandage on their heads in the colour of their choice and they can even have stickers on it. It looks like a very happy place to be, but to the parents this is the living hell they never wanted to experience.

Off the hall there are four single rooms for the children who are most ill, some of whom are just newborn babies. There are also three larger rooms with two and three beds in them. You know your child is getting better and is on the way to discharge when they are accommodated here, because these rooms are at the end of the corridor furthest from the nurses' station.

In two weeks' time it is Valentine's Day. The play specialist has been making beautiful heart shaped cards with the children, with smaller red hearts, roses and pink fluffy bits stuck on. The kids will give these to each other, the nurses and their loved ones. The patients have also been writing love poems on a laptop the nurses bought for the ward from the proceeds of a sponsored pub-crawl. The ward secretary prints out the poems and the children glue them into their Valentine cards.

On the nurses' desk is a novelty phone in the shape of Mickey Mouse, with his ears for the receiver and the numbers on his tummy. All the children get to phone home. It is breathtaking to hear them laugh – they all have had or are going to have brain surgery. I find myself looking at the phone that brings so much happiness to the children, and contemplating that it yet may bring me the worst news I could ever imagine.

I hear my name mentioned.

What's going on, this isn't long enough, is he dead? Why are they looking for me?

I don't know whether to shout loudly to let them know where I am or be silent. Maybe they will go away if I stay quiet. But what if Stephen has woken up suddenly with a fright and is calling out, asking for his mummy?

The nurse puts her head round the doorway; her hair is falling untidily over her shoulders and she looks harassed.

"Mrs. Coombe, I have been looking all over the place for you, up and down the hospital and in and out of the ward. Would you like some lunch?"

9

The time, not surprisingly, has moved at snail's pace.

It is now 2pm, Monday 1 February 1999, and the nurses have changed shift for this afternoon. They work in two 12-hour shifts per day, each nurse doing four shifts a week. This arrangement is quite difficult to deal with, as you tend to bond with a nurse and then don't see her until the following week.

The ward is bustling with visitors. Some parents have brought along their other children and members of their families. A grandmother has cooked a large tray of roast chicken for her young daughter who has a baby in the ward. This girl is a first time mother, and you can see the anxiety in her face. I wonder what the gran is thinking as she tries to comfort her own daughter, while the daughter in turn settles her new baby.

The delicious smell of the chicken is wafting through

the ward. It is easy to imagine licking your fingers and tasting the salty sticky skin. The gran has made a jumbo lot and insists that the other parents share in this delight. It is almost tempting for a moment.

Sisters and brothers are bringing gifts, flowers and balloons to their sick siblings, and cheering their mothers who stay in the ward with lots of wonderful hugs and kisses. Husbands embrace wives, offering them much needed reassurance.

I watch all this from the sidelines, alone, and with a perennial pain in my heart. The man I married 18 years ago, the man who said he would be with me forever, is not sharing this agony with me today. He is unreachable for me. I feel a pang of regret that I asked my parents not to come today. I am trying to be the strong one and protect everyone else from this trauma. I want them to see I have the love and strength to deal with this. Yet my sorrow is unbearable. I cannot even see the foe I am fighting.

One of the nurses, Sister Granville, comes to Stephen's room where I sit, and gently knocks on the door. She has come to inform me that they are going to need this room for another sick child. The news makes me feel that Stephen is no longer a concern of theirs, worsening my mood.

Do they not have any feelings? Worse, do they know Stephen is not coming back to this ward and are not telling me?

Sister Granville asks me to pack up all Stephen's belongings and put them into his bedside cabinet, then put the cabinet into the cupboard at the end of the ward.

I look at Stephen's belongings, the little things that make him so special. I take his pillow, the last one his little head rested upon. I am not giving the pillowslip back to the nurses. On it I can see his fine blond hairs and smell the sweet scent of his bubble bath, lotion and talc. The last thing we did together last night was to run a lovely warm bubble bath, and as he played with his bath toys I sat smiling at him, my heart tearing.

The children's ward has a security door whose access code is known only by medical staff. Visitors must ring a doorbell to be let in, for safety reasons and to make sure none of the patients leave or are taken from the ward without a nurse's permission. The ward across the corridor beyond this door is no longer in use due to NHS cutbacks, so parents are allowed to sleep in the empty beds while their children are critically ill.

I was shown to a side room next to the unused ward. This room was originally designed to be used by one patient, but now two old hospital beds are squeezed into it. There is barely 12 inches between the beds; if you sit on the side of one bed your knees will touch the other. The two empty beds retain the remnants of the discoloured plastic covering used to repel spillages, covered by a white sheet. A sickening aroma permeates the room.

On opening the door the first thing you see is a dirty old plastic chair. This chair used to be bright orange but now it resembled a lopsided brown and blue heap of junk, with one leg so bent that the seat tilts about an inch to one side. Unless you fancy a spine rattling time I would avoid this chair.

Off the room is a kind of an en-suite facility – that's if you can count a dingy, smelly bathroom with no light working. I suppose this is to conceal the hard brown toilet paper. It is like the kind of paper you used to get in school in the 70s, which I remember using to do tracing work in geography. Thank God another person has left some unused man-size tissues behind!

The window...well, how can I describe this? There are no blinds or curtains of any kind, and it has a large crack that lets in the wind and light, preventing you from getting any sleep. I think this must be a ploy to keep parents awake in case their child needs comfort or feeding during the nurses' break time, or on night shift when they might be sleeping!

The door has a window in the centre taking up almost half of its area, and on the outside of the window there is a blind. I thought at first it was a bit strange that the blind can only be closed from the corridor side, and then I remembered that this was so the nurses could check patients inside the room. I wanted to be left alone, and did not want anyone passing this room to be able to pry into my sorrow. So I took a sheet from one of the beds, neatly folded it lengthwise avoiding the hole in the middle and the threadbare bits, opened the door, slung the sheet over the top, and closed the door tight.

Through the window I could see that what had started out a beautiful bright February day was now a raging storm. The skies were dark and empty, just like my arms. Tall bare trees blew sideways so far that they looked in danger of uprooting. Pieces of paper swirled around, clogging roadside drains, and a large puddle had formed directly in my view. The little school children now on their way home splashed in and out of it. Some of the children had no wellies, and their tiny feet were getting very wet.

Why aren't their mothers taking better care of them? If Stephen was out in this storm, he would be wrapped up like a Christmas turkey with no room for wind or water to get to him.

I notice a small-framed old lady struggling to make it to the bus stop. Her umbrella has been torn from her grasp by the wind, her headscarf is blowing in front of her face, and I can imagine the stinging of the wind on her cheeks. Luckily, a young lad ties his dog to a lamp post and comes to her rescue.

I am hugging Stephen's pillow, crying quietly to myself and rocking back and forth. I must have cried myself to sleep. Suddenly, I wake to the sound of a child's cry, feeling numb and confused. It takes me a few seconds to remember where I am.

I turn round on the bed and sit against the wall with Stephen's pillow resting on my lap. I can feel the iciness of the wall on my back, almost burning it is so cold, but I can't be bothered to move. I notice that the floor of this room was once pale green shiny marble but now the gloss has been worn off by years of cleaning. The corners, where no polishing machines could reach, are a brownish colour.

As I sit there, my contemplation roaming about the room, I am drawn to a little silvery coloured spider slowly crawling up the wall beside the broken window. I don't know what kind of spider it is; in any case, I didn't realise there were any about in the winter. Perhaps it is my imagination playing tricks on me.

I am startled by a knock on the door. Before I have a chance to say anything or get up the door slowly opens. A cheeky smiling face pops from behind the door – my younger brother, Greg.

He says, "I know you told everyone you would be OK here today on your own, but as I was sitting at my desk thinking of you, I knew had to come and make sure you and little Stephen were OK."

This tender sentiment brings me to tears, but for once they are not sad tears, they're loving ones. My young brother thinks enough of me to come to my aid when I most need it.

Greg has a difficult time trying to talk me in to going to the tearoom for some lunch, but I eventually give in, even if it is only to keep him from nagging. I go round to the nurses' station to let them know where I am going in case anything should happen to Stephen.

My brother stays with me for about an hour before he must return to work. It was a very difficult goodbye, as neither of us knew what to say. So we just hugged for a moment before he left.

Shortly after I get back to the ward, my husband appears on his lunch break. He sits on the bed opposite me but we don't talk. I know if I say anything it will start an argument, and I am not in the mood, nor do I have the energy for one. Not while my little one is fighting for his life. I want to keep all my thoughts focused on him.

After a short time Stephen's father leaves. He says only that he will come back in the evening.

The time is now 3pm. I have watched the clock in this

room go round every hour until I am dizzy. Stephen has been in surgery for over seven hours now.

What stage are they at?

The length of time must be a good sign: since they hadn't contacted me yet, I permit myself the hopeful assumption that things are going to plan.

But how long can I sit here twiddling my thumbs?

I decide to leave my small prison, and go down the roasting corridor to the nurses' station. I am going to ask them to phone down to the operating room and see if they can glean some information on Stephen's progress.

Yet, when I get up to make my foray, I find I am too frightened to leave my cocoon. It is as if I have been in this room for an eternity. I pace up and down. I go to the door and open it then go back and sit on the edge of the bed. When I pass the mirror I see a face I do not recognise; the eyes and nose are swollen and red, and tears stain the face.

At 8.30pm Mr. Hyde and his assistant come to the ward. My husband is still waiting with me, and we all go to the doctor's room to hear the outcome of the surgery.

Mr. Hyde starts by telling us that Stephen has made it

through the surgery and is in the process of being made ready to go to intensive care. I am flooded with indescribable relief.

He continues: "I was able to remove about 90 percent of the tumour, but in doing so I have caused some brain damage. I knew it would not have been possible in such a difficult operation not to damage something. I have removed what I think to be the safest amount and still preserve a good quality of life. There is a paralysis on Stephen's left side and his right eye will not stay open. I think I have cut through the muscle that holds the eye open. I will let you know when the staff in ICU are ready to take you to visit Stephen. I am now going to get in touch with Dr Donaldson, the endocrinologist, and I will inform him of Stephen's situation. I know he has quite a bit of work to do and will be in touch with you soon."

A short time later a nurse comes to take us to see Stephen in intensive care.

10

We leave the children's ward and go down to room 62 on the second floor, the intensive care unit. My mind is buzzing with questions.

What will he look like? Will I recognise him? Will he recognise me? Will he be in pain? Will there be blood, and will I see the scar on his beautiful head?

A family is gathered in a side room, some of them crying hysterically, others cuddling and comforting their distraught relations. I feel sympathy, but am also unnerved.

Is this what we should be doing? Oh God! I'm too scared to go and see my baby.

I leave this room as I don't want to intrude in the family's grief. I wait in the corridor for a nurse to take me to Stephen when he is ready and settled. My husband, by contrast, remains in the room, impervious to the family's distress.

Stephen's bed in the intensive care unit is beside the window. The curtains around him have been drawn shut because the young girl in the next bed apparently has only a short time to live. It is this girl's family who we encountered in the waiting room. I hope Stephen and I are spared this trauma.

A nurse arrives to take me to my son. I slowly walk over to his bed. I am quite amazed at how normal he looks: although he has a massive turban bandage on his head he looks peaceful, as if he is sound asleep. I pray he is dreaming of lovely things and not the events of 12 hours ago. I reach out to touch him. I tenderly kiss his forehead and hold his little hand.

My sweet baby, what have I let them do to you?

An array of tubes comes from his head into a large blood filled plastic bag by the bedside. Another drain emerges from his groin into a second bag. There are ECG pads on his chest. A network of coloured wires attaches him to various monitors on either side of the bed. On the wall behind him is a large bank of 12 electrical points. Seven sockets are used by the machines keeping Stephen alive. The multiple lines form a barrier like a spider's web that I cannot break through.

To my surprise a male cleaner comes to Stephen's bedside and starts to work. As he goes about cleaning he stirs up dust. I can't help but wonder if this is safe to do. The man gives me an uncomfortable smile, and then gets on with his work.

A nurse approaches me to quietly explain all the unfamiliar technology. She whispers: "The tube that is coming out of the turban is draining the blood from around his brain into this bag. The smaller tubes in his arms and legs are being used to administer the medication he needs. The pads on his chest tell us his heart rate, blood pressure, the oxygen level in his blood, and that everything is going well."

The nurse confirms what the surgeon had already told me: Stephen is paralysed on his right side and his left eye doesn't open properly. She says that they hope that this would be temporary, and tells me that the surgeon will visit later to answer any other questions I might have.

Around this time, Stephen's dad comes to his bedside and holds his hand for a moment. He quickly leaves. He did not even look at me, let alone say anything to me.

The surgeon comes to see us an hour later. He tells me that Stephen might suffer from diabetes insipidus, an adrenal hormone deficiency in which the body produces excessive urine, causing the patient to seriously dehydrate. They need to do a 24-hour fluid balance on Stephen, which meant they would have to fit a urinary catheter.

This is an adult hospital, and although I don't know a great deal about medical equipment, I realise quickly and to my horror that they only have adult size catheters. They attempt to insert the too-big catheter, a procedure that was cruel in the extreme, leaving Stephen squirming and in severe pain. Seeing my child like this I beg them to let me go to the children's hospital and collect a children's catheter of the correct size for Stephen. Their response to my appeal is to escort me from the room, so that I can hear my son screaming from outside.

As it happens, the family of the dying girl in the bed next to Stephen sees me and they kindly offer support. I wonder what they think about me being alone, when there were so many of them to comfort each other.

After a while, I don't know how long, a nurse comes out to take me in to Stephen. They had put him to sleep to push the enormous catheter in, but even after the excruciating pain and suffering he had to endure, they had failed. Finally, they had resorted to a female catheter that they stuck with heavy-duty tape around his groin.

For three days and nights I sat beside my baby watching every breath he took. I dared not leave his side for a minute in case he woke and I was not there. I had promised I would always be there for him and intended to keep my word. Sometimes he would whimper in his sleep, and I would wonder if he could remember the horrors that had gone before.

As for his father, he would visit outside the visiting-time schedule, staying only for a few minutes each time. He would never talk to me. I tried, especially when Stephen was awake, to speak to his dad, but I was simply ignored.

During this time my parents brought Sam and Kirsty to visit Stephen. I was ever so pleased to see them. I made a point of being very honest about Stephen's condition and tried to answer frankly Kirsty's frequent questions about all the tubes and lines coming and going from his body. The best thing of all was that Kirsty and Sam's visit gave me a chance to hug them, and reconnect after all the time I had had to concentrate my energies on Stephen.

Laughter in the ICU is very rare. But one day, Stephen suddenly sat bolt upright and said, "I'm hungry." The nursing staff were amazed. They all gathered around his bed and chatted animatedly to him. Stephen, for his part, was talking at one hundred miles an hour. One nurse giggled and said, "I think he has been saving up all his chatting and it's all coming out at once." Medically, the rapid-fire chatter was a product of the brain's post-operative healing process, during which signals get confused.

Stephen was quite adamant he was hungry. So the staff called down to the kitchen and asked for food for a patient to be brought to ward 62. The kitchen staff laughed and asked if the nurses were joking. They knew that ward 62 is the ICU, where no patients are ever well enough to eat.

The nurse reassured the kitchen lady that they had a hungry little boy who had just woken up from brain surgery. A short time later a porter brought Stephen the meal he'd requested: burger, chips and ice cream. He sat up eagerly and ate all the food as if he had never been fed before. I watched in astonishment, but didn't realise then that his voracious hunger was going to prove to be such a difficult thing to manage later.

On the morning of Stephen's last day in ICU, day three after the operation, one of my friends came to visit. I met her downstairs and told her not to worry about what she might see, because Stephen was quite stable. We waited outside ICU for the nurse to answer the doorbell, a measure to ensure the patients' privacy and dignity was respected.

When we got in we went straight over to Stephen's bed. He was sitting up chatting to the nurse. Stephen was telling her how much money he had saved up and that he wanted to take her out on a date. I turned to my friend and the look of horror on her face was a sight to see. The nurses had just removed Stephen's turban bandage to reveal the row of metal staples holding his head together. I had to take a second look for myself. No one had told me this was what was under the bandage. Stephen said excitedly, "Mummy, look at my head. The doctor used his staple gun to hold my scar together. Isn't it great?"

I was numb.

For the next couple of days Stephen was able to stay awake for longer periods, and would often ask me to massage him with lavender oil, something that I had done to relieve his pain when he was younger. The nurses were always joking about this and kidding Stephen that they were going to take him out of his bed, put him into a chair, hop into his bed and take turns for me to massage their feet.

We enjoyed many laughs about this, and it was welcome light relief.

11

Thursday 4 February. Day three after the operation.

We go back to the children's ward. Stephen is put into one of the single rooms next to the nurses' station reserved for very sick children. Now that the tight turban bandage had been removed, his head and face are beginning to swell and go black and blue. For the first time in his battle with this tumour he looks like a sick child. To add to his woes, he is in severe pain.

Stephen had been lying still for several days now, so his lungs had not been doing much work. It was important to get them working or pneumonia, which can be fatal, could set in. The physiotherapist was visiting him three times in a 24-hour period to help him cough. The exercises he had to do caused him great pain in his head. I sat for many hours holding a cold cloth to his forehead to ease his suffering, but nothing was working.

His dad's visits were also becoming a great strain. He limited them now to once a day at 7am before work, staying for about ten to 15 minutes each time. There was clearly someone telling him not to visit. Stephen naturally wanted his dad to visit more often. He'd say, "Mum, all the other kids have their dads with them, why can't my dad come and stay with me all day?" I always had to make excuses for him.

On Thursday 4 February, day four after surgery, things came to a head.

It started well with words of comfort and a gentle arm around my shoulders. A nurse sees my pain and is aware of the difficult time I am having with my husband.

She says: "Look Irene, today you've three beautiful children that you might not have had, so look on the bright side. There are many people who can't have children or whose children die in surgery. Stephen has pulled through. Put your thoughts into him and your other two children. Do not let your husband's problems take that from you and them. Be strong, as I know you can. We are here to help. Please let us."

Later, I see my husband through the glass doors as he arrives.

Here we go again. What will it be today: another argument or the silent treatment? Oh surprise,

Stephen's dad has brought him a gift. Ha ha, we should know by now not to get excited.

My husband approaches Stephen, bends down to him and passes over his offering. I glance at my friends who are visiting this evening, and understand the look on their faces without any words passing between us. A lousy book, free from a tea bag packet – this is the degree of affection and forethought this man brings to his sick child.

Unusually, he now addresses me. He says that he has brought some clean clothes for Stephen, but has left the in the boot of the car. I am only too eager to offer to go to the car park and get them, with my friends in tow, as they do not wish to spend any longer in my husband's company.

The wind howls and freezing sleet falls on me as I make my way to the car, which could not be further from the hospital door if he'd tried. But my son needs clean pyjamas, even if it is too much for his dad to retrieve them. With numb fingers and blinded by the sleet, I manage to open the car door. I notice that on the dashboard is a pair of spectacles, and I know who they belong to. I was initially told there was no other person involved with my husband, but here, alone in the dark, I find out that that was a lie.

The crushing sound beneath my feet is pleasurable in the extreme.

What will *one do with no glasses to see through?*

How tempting the catering skip looks to me right now. Scattering the glass across the car park I take the frames and dump them, as I was dumped, into the skip. If only for a minute or two I feel satisfied.

Frozen to the bone now, and cheeks ruby red from the cold, I am back at my son's bedside.

My husband says he must leave.

"*Really?* If you must go we don't mind," I say smugly, relishing my knowledge of the surprise he has in store when he gets back to the car.

I smile like the Cheshire cat that got the cream.

If I knew of the consequences of my act of sabotage, however, I would have left the glasses just where they were.

It is amazing how quickly one can climb six flights of stairs when one is very angry. The look on my husband's face when he arrived back in Stephen's room was an amalgam of anger and pure hatred. If I was alone I would have been frightened for my life.

"What have you done with the glasses that were in my car?" he whispered, his voice harsh with barely suppressed fury.

Under the circumstances, I opt for a lie: " I don't know what you are talking about. Anyway, visiting time is over and you have to go."

I doubt, at this moment, that I could cope with an outburst. Thankfully, he leaves and I can turn my attention again on my baby and try to calm down.

An hour or so later another mum and I go to the front door of the hospital for some fresh air while our children are sleeping. I decide to call my parents and tell them that Stephen is coming along fine, and I will see them tomorrow. As I hang up, my mobile phone rings. When I answer, the screams from my angry husband penetrate the night air. The other mothers hear them and look away embarrassed.

"What have you done with the glasses? You are in big trouble now, you wait and see. Where are the glasses, where are the glasses!?"

Stunned, I opt again for the lie and plead innocent. Excuses come from nowhere. I tell the other mothers I would like some time on my own and they politely leave. I am frightened by my husband at this moment in a way that I have never been before. In 18 years he never as much as raised his voice, and now he is yelling dreadful threats. I don't know what to do.

I decide to head for the skip. In the sleet and piercing wind I stretch to reach into its murky depths and search with frozen hands for the glasses I dumped earlier.

I am bursting with emotion. My brain hurts and tears blur my vision.

Why does everything have to be so complicated?

All the other couples in the children's ward seem so loving, and I am out in the freezing cold searching through a skip for something I do not want to find for someone I don't want to know. In the pitch dark, unsurprisingly, I cannot find the glasses. My heart races with anxiety at the prospect that my husband may return to the hospital.

Trembling, I call home. He answers.

"Can I speak to Kirsty?" I ask, trying to sound calm.

"NO!"

"Don't be silly, let me talk to Kirsty or Sam."

"NO!"

In the background I can hear Kirsty pleading with her father to let her speak to me, but he is unmoved. Then, he hangs up the phone on me. Repeatedly I redial, but he has now switched off the phone.

I blame myself for my predicament. If I had not been so selfish in my impetuous act my kids would be able to chat to me, and I could wish them goodnight.

The next day is Friday 5 February. My eyes are puffy and I have a blinding headache, but these maladies bear no comparison to what I am about to suffer.

Stephen's father and I sit on opposite sides of Stephen's bed. I chose to sit on the other side advisedly – I want to protect myself from my husband's wrath. I notice a small cut on his head and ask him what happened and if he is OK. His reply will never leave me.

With his arm outstretched and his hand open close to my face, he utters the words forever inscribed in my memory:

"Stephen will die and you are to blame. You are evil, the devil, and all that is going wrong is your fault. You do not exist in my world, and I do not intend to speak to you ever again. Do not speak to me."

The contemptuous look on his face tells me that, incredibly, he is serious.

After he leaves, I collect myself as best I can so as to attend to Stephen.

12

At lunchtime Friday 5 February, four days post-op, the nurses and I manage to get Stephen onto a large comfy chair where he could eat his meal. This was the first time since Monday's surgery that he had been out of bed and he was very happy, even though he still had to contend with multiple tubes and lines.

Just after lunch Stephen drops off to sleep and I read a magazine to distract myself from my husband's extraordinary outburst. Surely it is all the stress of the situation that is upsetting him, and he will come around later to apologise for his ferocious words.

Due to the seriousness of Stephen's surgical needs, his operation took place in an adult hospital. The vital instructions for his post-operative endocrine treatment have been given over the telephone from the children's hospital.

Stephen is receiving a medication called DDAVP or desmopresin, which controls a hormone that regulates urine production and assists fluid balance.

Bloods have to be taken every four hours for testing, and sometimes the results were a bit late in coming back, making it difficult to administer the correct amount of medication. It is also increasingly difficult for Dr Donaldson, the specialist endocrinologist based at the kids' hospital, to treat Stephen long-distance, so he makes many journeys from the children's to us to check on Stephen's progress. He comes before his clinic in the morning at the children's hospital, after his shift finished around teatime, and late in the evening. He also made numerous phone calls during the day to check Stephen's pathology. Dr Donaldson juggled these responsibilities for Stephen with caring for numerous other patients and, to my gratitude, was always happy to explain Stephen's condition.

It's now 2pm. Visiting time is here, and I wake Stephen as his gran and sister have arrived. This is the first time Stephen cannot be roused.

I leave his room to find the nurse.

She tells me sharply to "give him a chance to wake. He has had major brain surgery," she says, "and you are just panicking for nothing. I will come and see him in a while."

I return to Stephen's room. The look on my mother's face will never leave me. She points at Stephen. He is biting his lip so hard that it is beginning to bleed, and his eyes are rolling back in his head. She is trying not to alarm Kirsty, but insists I go back and get the nurse.

I try to talk to him, but he is unresponsive and staring into space. I ask my mum to take Kirsty to the shop for something to drink so that I can get help for Stephen. I don't want Kirsty to see anything upsetting.

I put the sides up around his bed and go to look for a nurse again. They are in the sisters' room having their lunch. This is normal practice, as at this time the patients all have visitors and the nursing staff don't like to do any procedures.

I pop my head into the sister's room. I am waiting for another telling off, and I start to cry as I tell them I think something is wrong with Stephen. One nurse, Jane, immediately jumps up and comes with me to Stephen's room. To my surprise she instantly pulls the pillows from under his head and bangs on the alarm on the wall. She yells at me to go and fetch another nurse immediately.

I find another nurse, Marie, and tell her that Jane wants her. She is busy at this moment trying to take a blood sample from another patient, and calls to Jane that she will be there when she is finished.

By this time I am back in Stephen's room. With extreme urgency in her voice, Jane asks me to hand over a tube that is on a shelf on the wall. I don't know what they are so I just grab all of the tubes and throw them onto Stephen's bed. At this point Marie comes in and Jane shouts at her to call the crash team.

I now see Jane putting a tube down Stephen's throat. He is not resisting. I finally realise something is very wrong. Stephen is beginning to convulse, shaking vigorously as the spasms quickly get more severe. He is about to bounce off the bed. I stand there, silent and in deep shock, as Jane says, "You should leave the room now."

I refuse. "After what my baby has come through," I tell her, "I will be beside him even if it is the end. I told Stephen I would never leave him and I won't."

Suddenly he stops all movement and turns blue. Stephen has just died in front of me.

Jane jumps onto his bed and begins resuscitation. At last, the ICU crash team arrives and takes over from Jane.

An auxiliary nurse comes into the room and starts to remove everything that is not fastened to the floor. She literally throws out the chairs, fan, table, TV, lunch tray and my belongings.

With fear in her eyes she says, "Come with me and we will call Stephen's dad at work. I think he should get here quickly."

"No, I want to call my brother," I say. "He is the one I rely on."

As we move from Stephen's room to the staff room to make the call I can see my mum and Kirsty outside the door through the glass panel. I gesture to them that everything is all right.

When I call my brother I do not need to say much. We had agreed earlier that if I called him at work it would mean I needed him here, now.

After I hang up the phone, the nurse asks me for permission to call my husband at work. I agree; I cannot deprive him of seeing his son under these circumstances.

It is not long before my husband arrives, as his work is close to the hospital. Our terrible argument, during which he had accused me of being evil and the cause of Stephen's illness and possible imminent death, had occurred only that morning. When Stephen went into crisis in the afternoon I was beginning to think he was correct.

That was until he arrived. I saw him coming through the door and went directly over to him, putting my arms out to give and receive a hug. But he stepped back and said, "I want nothing to do with you. Remember, you do not exist in my world."

He then proceeded towards Stephen's room. Fortunately, at that moment my brother arrived, and I received the support I so much needed.

At this stage, the nursing staff and doctors had stopped running into Stephen's room. I thought, this was this because he was dead or better.

All at once, my dad and sisters arrived and joined my mother and daughter outside the ward.

It was now 5pm. Three hours had passed so quickly. By chance, Dr Donaldson had learned of Stephen's fit in a phone call to the ward. He rushed over to the hospital to assess the situation. The neurosurgeon had also arrived, and reassured me that Stephen's crying in pain, as he was doing now, was an indication that he had pretty good brain function.

I went out to the waiting area and explained all that had transpired to my family and told them not to worry; everything would be okay. I asked my parents to take Sam and Kirsty home, and my sister if she would drive my car there. I asked my husband to take Stephen's belongings – his clothes, toys and gifts – home to my house, and with a strained expression he agreed.

I was now back in the room alone with my baby. He had a thick tube coming from his nose, and had been wired up to the same machines he was on in the ICU. He was coming in and out of consciousness, and every couple of minutes he would spasm. Periodically he cried out for me and said that it hurt. Once again I was looking at my baby in pain, and, once again, I could not ease his suffering.

I felt helpless. The doctor had said that they had given Stephen enough anticonvulsant medication to keep a horse down. I had asked them why he was still convulsing. They replied that it was to do with triggers in the brain firing after the surgery, and told me that it would settle down soon.

The two doctors had stepped out to confer about the next stage of treatment, and how best to help Stephen. They decided to make sure Stephen was stable and then transfer him to the children's hospital. After the terrible trauma of watching my son die in front of me, and witnessing the medical staff's frantic efforts to revive him, we were now to move.

Before we left the neuro hospital a special paediatric registrar came to see us and assess Stephen. She had to confirm that he was stable enough to make the journey. She seemed to be a very young girl of about 20, and I began worrying when she could not fit the cables to the electrocardiograph. I left the room to ask a nurse if this doctor knew what she was doing, as she didn't seem very confident to me. The nurse said I was to stop worrying and go and tend to Stephen.

About an hour and a half later the ambulance team came to collect us, and after the two male paramedics filled in multiple forms, we left for our journey to the children's.

A funny thing happened on our way out the hospital. As we were going down to ground level, the lift broke down. Luckily, none of us was agoraphobic. Instead, we laughed. One of the paramedics said that this has happened to them before, and I was not to worry as they had enough equipment to go to the Himalayas and back.

13

Friday 5 February 1999.

On arrival at the children's hospital, Stephen is immediately taken to the ICU. Dr Donaldson and his specialist endocrine nurse are waiting. I am allowed to be with him for a short time and then a nurse shows me to a ward that has an extra bed for me to sleep in overnight if I wish.

When I return to the ICU Dr Donaldson takes me aside into a waiting room. He gently updates me on Stephen's condition:

"Stephen's life is in grave danger at the moment and we need to find the correct balance of medication to help save him. I was hoping this would not happen, but this is the difficulty we face with the patients needing treatment in two different hospitals. Now that Stephen is here I can watch over him more closely and check his bloods hourly, and this will make for a vast improvement in his treatment."

Immediately, I feel reassured that we were in the right place. My feelings are confirmed when I see the difference the paediatric medical staff have made to Stephen already. They have been able to insert a catheter into his bladder without him suffering any discomfort – a catheter that was the right size for his body. They have also inserted an arterial line into his arm to monitor all his vital signs. It is not that the staff in the adult hospital did not care for Stephen – in fact, the treatment was generally second to none. It is just that they lacked the correct tools to do the job.

At last, for a fleeting moment, everything seemed to be going smoothly for Stephen.

I am able to stay with him as long as I wish, but the nurses did a great job of reassuring me that he would be fine under their care, and I eventually go to the ward and sleep for a short time.

I reflect on how two different family tragedies have coincided: on the one hand my husband has betrayed me, and on the other, my child is struggling to live. Through this, Dr Donaldson is trying to keep us together in our focus on Stephen. He asks my husband to come to the hospital, and they have a chat about what is happening to our son.

At this time, as my husband tried to break free from our marriage, I found out that he has asked my children to deceive me. When Sam visits the next day – while his little brother is still fighting for his life – he tells me something that he knows will get him into trouble with his father. My husband has won a terrific amount of money on the lottery, an amazing £6000, and has warned Sam that he must not let me know this. Fearfully, Sam begs me not to tell his dad that he has divulged this secret.

Using a child in this way must be criminal. But my son knows the right thing to do. He knows it is his father's responsibility to make sure his family is provided for, and this is his reason for bringing the win to my attention.

Nevertheless, I am stunned by the news. I am here at the hospital with no money to feed myself, buy a coke, make a phone call or give my kids pocket money. My husband, on the other hand, is out shopping, making sure he is all right.

Does he not realise the love and respect my children have for me?

Mum, dad and all of us.
November 1999

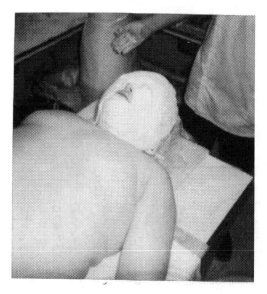

Stephen getting his plaster of paris mask made for Radiotherapy treatment. May 2000

Stephen on his trip with the Police in
Jan 1999.

Stephen with Mr Charles Kinsey

14

After three days in children's hospital ICU we are moved to new ward.

A male nurse, Donald, begins to admit us. But after a short while another nurse comes to say Stephen is to be moved to the ward across the corridor.

Stephen has arterial lines in both wrists, a urinary catheter, and he is naked, as we have come direct from ICU. In addition to this, he is as yet not fully conscious or lucid. He is very confused and sees things that don't exist. He is still in this state as we are moved from ward to ward.

In the new ward, we are put into the end bed bay with eight beds. The ward is large and full of rowdy kids. The general wards at the children's hospital, such as this one, have no limit on visitor numbers or visiting times.

As we entered the ward, all the kids and their visitors had a good look, and some had a laugh at Stephen's expense.

In the bed facing Stephen there is a little cheeky-looking boy with pyjamas that don't quite fit. The legs are at half-mast and some of the buttons on his top are missing. He has red wiry hair, freckles on his face and chocolate smudged all over his mouth. There is an older version of this boy sitting on a chair playing a game. What came out of his mouth will stay with me forever, and has become a story told at family reunions and parties.

"Hey, look at that wee guy o'er there," he said excitedly, "he's got a zip across his heed and two black eyes. He must've hud a fight wi' Frank Bruno! Hey missus, cannae unzip his heed so that we can see his brains fa' oot!"

All the children turned round simultaneously to see who had said this. The boy's mother gave him such a slap on his ear that it must have been ringing for days.

I have had enough. When the nurse came to introduce herself, I told her Stephen could not stay in this ward. I ask to talk to someone in charge. The ward sister comes and I bring to her attention that fact that his arterial lines are dislodged and blood is flowing back up them. Worse, Stephen has just come from ICU with an open wound on his head and has been put into a ward with children with meningitis. I tell her that this is unacceptable and I want my baby to be put into a side room away from the danger of infection and prying eyes.

Eventually, after many phone calls, the sister reaches Dr Donaldson. He is eager to acknowledge my worries and gives the OK for Stephen to be moved. They put Stephen in a single room at the exit of the ward, which unfortunately is not much better.

Dr Donaldson insists Stephen has 24-hour care, and the ward sister eventually secures an agency nurse. I was thus able to leave him at around 2am to have a short sleep. At 6am, I was back on the ward for his next blood test. His little face was a study in fear when they came at him with the needles.

Things were swinging from one extreme to the other, Dr Donaldson said,. The fluctuations in Stephen's hormones had to be controlled, as they were very dangerous.

"Stephen is still a very sick child, and this is life threatening," he warned.

Dr Donaldson now decides to take blood samples hourly again, and it wasn't long before Stephen ran out of useful veins. On a number of occasions we had to wait while they got a neonatologist to take

Stephen's blood, as he was more adept at finding smaller veins. His expertise is with tiny helpless newborn babies. Once, when there were no more veins available, the endocrine nurse had to collect blood by pricking all Stephen's little swollen fingertips and toes and gently squeezing it drop by drop into a little test tube.

Night two in the children's ward, and, as I was not told otherwise, I foolishly expect another agency nurse. I feel it is safe for me to try to get a little sleep just as I did the night before, so I leave Stephen and head off to bed. When I get back to the ward in the morning, a nurse abruptly tells me Stephen has been left alone all night without an agency nurse, and has fallen out of bed twice. She says this is unacceptable as they had other patients to tend to, and that it had annoyed them as it disturbed their tea break. I was asked not to leave Stephen during the night in case this happened again. Apparently, they thought I was a robot that needed no rest or sleep.

As the long weeks go by I begin to notice that the nurses prefer the little, cute babies. When they compared my son, with his distressing eating disorder and emerging behavioural problems, with the infants, the latter always won.

There were also differences in treatment according the background of the child, and the appearance of the parents. On one sad occasion a little baby boy from a very poor background was admitted. He was being sick frequently, and it didn't take long for the nurses to get a bit fed up with him. Their attitude quickly changed from tender care to contempt. At one point, this baby began to gag on his vomit. When I alerted the young female student doctor she looked at him in disgust and refused to touch him until he was cleaned up. It was very distressing for the other mums in the ward to witness, as we were concerned that the baby might asphyxiate. It made us aware, also, of what could happen to our children when we were not in the ward.

Because of these concerns, and the lack of competence of the nursing staff in caring for children with Stephen's condition – they had not had a case comparable to his before – I never left him unattended.

As time passed, my parents were the only support I had. None of my lifelong friends came to the hospital to give me any type of help. Only a new friend, Myra, and her daughter, Claire, came every evening. I really looked forward to their visits, especially as Myra was a former nurse and helped me to understand what was happening and what questions I needed to ask. Claire was a young nursing student, and always helped cheer up Stephen. I don't know how I would have managed with out their strength and loving support.

It had now been six weeks since Stephen's admission

to this ward, and I was exhausted. I had had close to no sleep or relaxation, and the strain was beginning to take its toll. One day as I was walking down the corridor to go to the canteen I felt quite dizzy and faint. There was no way I was going to tell anyone, so I found a toilet and sat there for over an hour sipping from the water tap until I felt I was able to continue.

I cannot explain where I got the strength, but I think when a mother knows her child is in great need of her special love and caring she will find an abundance of Inner resources.

During his stay in this ward, I was reluctant to complain about Stephen's care or lack of it, in case the nurses became resentful towards him. So I said nothing. I felt I had no choice but to bite my lip and just pray for the time Stephen would be well enough to leave the hospital and go home.

Around this time, my parents came to my rescue again and offered to stay with Stephen to let me have a break.

One afternoon I hear my dad praying at Stephen's bedside. Through his tears, he offers himself to God in Stephen's place: "Please take me instead of my grandson. I have lived a full and long life. Stephen does not deserve to suffer like this."

My new friends, Myra and Clair also see the strain I

am enduring after many weeks of being with Stephen in hospital, and arrange for me to go on a short break with them to Dublin. They'd held a special evening in our local pub to raise money for me for this surprise trip. The forthcoming Saturday, they had organised for the presentation of the funds to me at the pub. I was not planning to go out as I was too exhausted and skint, so my friends had to tell my parents of their plans so that they would talk me into going.

As we stand at our usual place the DJ calls my name and asks me to come to his corner. I can feel my face getting progressively redder as all the locals chant my name in unison. The DJ hands me an envelope containing over £600, and explains how the money was raised. Myra and my other friends had gathered raffle prizes, and convinced the publican to let them have the running of the pub for one night to sell raffle tickets, sing songs and almost anything else that would top up the collection tins.

I am so stunned I cannot even cry.

I was terrified to leave Stephen and go to Dublin for this short but much needed timeout. But his special nurse convinced me I needed the break, and that Stephen would be well looked after while I was away. I also made sure that my parents and brother were at hand to ensure Stephen was never left alone.

On my return to my relief I found that the world had

not suddenly fallen apart during my absence, and my three children had had a great time with their grandparents.

Batteries charged, I was ready for the next chapter.

15

The Malcolm Sergeant Charity provides the room I have been sleeping in since Stephen's second night in the children's hospital ward. They also have a purpose built house, more like a large hotel, at the bottom of the street from the hospital entrance. This facility is free for the parents of very sick children, and I now have a place there.

I am given a guided tour on my arrival with my dad and shown to my room. It has an en suite and two single beds. For peace of mind, there is also a telephone directly connected to the ICU, and parents are at liberty to phone the unit at any time of the day or night. The house also had a laundry room, and a spacious kitchen / dining room. Each guest has their own kitchen area complete with a cooker, cupboards, sink, and all the crockery and cutlery an average family would need, and there is a catering size fridge with an individual shelf for each family's groceries.

This house was a Godsend to me. I was very happy to be able to have Sam and Kirsty stay with me at times, while Stephen was still in the ward. It gave us a chance to be together without the distraction of Stephen.

Before Stephen was allowed home we were also able to trial him staying with me there. I could rest at ease because if anything went wrong I had the direct line to the ICU.

Dr Donaldson also needed to know if I could manage all of Stephens's medications before he would discharge him and this was the perfect place to learn. This arrangement also gave me the time and space to acquire the knowledge I would need. Day by day, Dr Donaldson and his team were educating me in Stephen's pituitary disorder. I had to understand the complexity of Stephen's medication and look for small signs of things going wrong. I was shown how to fill in his nursing charts and check his fluid balance.

Stephen's appetite was increasing daily, and I was always feeding him to try to build his strength so that I could get him home. One day, one of the children's hospital doctors, Dr King, took me aside and explained to me the grave problem of his appetite.

She said that while the brain surgery had been successful, and Dr Donaldson had balanced his life-saving medications, I now had to control Stephen's eating or he would eat himself to death. I was rattled by what she was saying, and didn't absorb the details. She gave me a booklet that had a fuller explanation, and I was able to study it at my leisure. It said that the hypothalamus – the part of the brain involved in Stephen's tumour – controls appetite. As Stephen's hypothalamus had been damaged in surgery when his tumour was removed, he does not know when to stop eating. In short, he never feels full. I hadn't fully realised until then that this was going to be a lifelong condition; I had assumed it was due to the high doses of steroids he had received during surgery.

The remainder of our days in the ward were full of laughter, and as Stephen was getting better his cheeky little smile was back. He had a hoot telling his awful jokes to the other children and their visitors. In fact he had become quite a celebrity in the ward.

We were now preoccupied, happily, with preparing Stephen for his discharge.

Physiotherapy was a big part of the process. Now *there* is an occupation you would have to have the patience of a saint to do! Children can be difficult when in pain, and none more so than Stephen. The expertise of the therapists was taken to the limit, but they managed not only to help him with his lungs but eventually to get him walking down seven flights of stairs.

The day before Stephen was to get home my mum and

I went to my house to prepare. My dad was left on duty looking after Stephen. Kirsty had been dividing her time between my parents' and my friend Jackie's place. Sam had been in our house with his dad while I stayed in the hospital. It was now over six weeks since I had been home.

The house felt so small and strange when I entered the front door. My mother and I were shocked to see the awful state it was in. I remember thinking I would need a week and an army of workers to make this place clean enough to bring my children home.

The first thing I noticed was the putrid smell of rotten oranges. I had encountered this stench before on a holiday, where the previous occupants of our hotel room had left fruit out of the fridge to go off. The fruit bowl in my kitchen resembled a sea of noxious green fungus, and it was the first thing we cleared.

The lounge was equally disastrous, littered with various fast food containers, plates, glasses, plastic bottles and wrappers of every kind. The kitchen looked like a bombsite.

We soon got down to cleaning. My house was an upstairs flat, so I had to make many journeys down the stairs to the bin shelter, adding to my cumulative exhaustion.

On top of all of this, there was a pile of dirty washing

you could hide a bus behind. We washed for hours, and by the evening all the clothes were ready to be bagged and taken to my mum's to dry, as I didn't have a tumble drier of my own.

I was very angry at the lack of care my husband had taken of the house. I had thought that, as he had spent so little time visiting Stephen at the hospital, he had ample time to keep the house in order. Also, my children were always taught to clear up after themselves and I did not appreciate the re-education in hygiene they were getting from their dad.

I know it was very difficult for my mum, but she didn't pass any comment about the terrible state of my house, or the fact that it was my husband who had allowed it to disintegrate into such disorder and filth.

What more would I have to put up with?

16

March 5 1999.

In many ways, it was a very special day – not only the day I brought Stephen home, but also my mum's birthday. For the first time in a long while we could let our hair down, try to relax and celebrate.

I have come through those painful days just gone; the isolation, the long, frightful hours and the searing pain in the pit of my stomach. I now look forward to a future with my child – a future that, only a few weeks ago, I was almost denied.

I am given a wheelchair to borrow by the physiotherapy team. We are off, home.

Earlier in the morning I had made many trips to the car, loading it with all our belongings. Stephen had gathered a mass of gifts, toys, cards and balloons from family and friends, and, in particular, from the local police force.

I was reminded that, last December, mum had gone to the local police station and told them about Stephen's impending surgery, and that he had always wanted to be a policeman when he grew up. The day before his admission, the police had taken him on an unforgettable journey, led by officer Jim Slack.

First, Stephen toured the local police station and was allowed to lock some officers, including Jim, into the cells. He then visited the mounted branch, where he helped to muck out and feed the horses, and the dog branch where he watched the dogs finding hidden drugs and helped feed and play with the new puppies. Then he was off to headquarters in the centre of Glasgow for lunch with the chief and his team. Finally, he was shown around the helicopter depot and inside the two helicopters.

You have never seen such a broad smile on the face of a child, and the joy was reciprocal. All through the day Stephen was bringing tears to the eyes of the tough officers with his little innocent remarks and his profuse thank-yous. The police even came to visit him in hospital dressed as the penguin-costumed Percy the policeman.

I hoped this magnificent day and the generous support of the local constabulary would be at the forefront of his mind during the unfolding trauma of his surgery and recovery.

At last the hour comes to go home. Stephen and I have a long walk through the hospital to the exit. All this time I am looking down at my little boy's scarred head, his arms and legs riddled with the puncture marks of all the needles he has had to endure.

I almost disbelieve that I am finally taking him home.

I wheel him through A&E towards the car park. The department is full of parents and children of all ages, some with injuries you can see and of course some like Stephen's that you cannot see. Some of the kids are screaming with pain, some are in wheelchairs, and there are some babies in prams. Some of the children seem quite carefree, running around playing with the toys. I wonder what could be their ailment?

The screen tells them that there is a four-hour wait to be seen. I have been here many times and waited many hours – I know how they must feel – but now, blessedly, I am going in the opposite direction. We are leaving.

I have tears in my eyes – tears that once stung and blinded me, but now represent a new beginning, and spring of from joy.

I feel like stopping and shouting at everyone to attract

their attention. "Look at us, we came here two months ago and my son was given a death sentence. I was told he would die or be a vegetable for the rest of his life, but look at him now. We are going home!"

I gently push Stephen through the dilapidated double doors to the outside world, of which we have been deprived for some weeks now. I suck in the fresh air deeply, filling my lungs to capacity. The sharpness of it stings but I am elated at the experience. I had forgotten the simple beauty of a spring morning in the sunshine-warmed open air.

Ahead is another journey to an unknown territory. Yes, our home is familiar, the neighbours the same as when we left, the river Clyde near our home still runs, but I have changed from a mother to a carer of a sick child. Or perhaps it is just that I have been caring for him all these years, and did not know how sick he was. Despite my joy at our homecoming, I feel fragile. My emotions are delicate, as If I might be shattered into many pieces by the slightest bump.

I know Stephen's condition will be paramount within our family's future.

I gently ease my son into the car, strap on his seatbelt, and cover him with a warm blanket. I recall that I have done this before, when I took Stephen, my last beautiful baby, home from the maternity hospital.

We leave the busy city streets and noise behind and drive along the dock road towards home. I keep looking over at Stephen. I hadn't allowed myself, I realise, not even for the shortest second, to believe that one day I would be taking him home all in one piece and in the best health possible.

His head is scarred, his little body now bloated with the side effects of his medication, and his skin shiny and stretched to bursting point, but his beautiful blue eyes sparkle with hope.

This is day one of our new life. The next twelve hours will be a challenge, but of a different order to the twelve excruciating hours of his surgery. I know I can manage; I have Sam and Kirsty to help me, and we are all together again.

What could be better?

17

It is now 2001, two years later. New problems have emerged.

Detached from all emotion and far removed from sanity, like a blood-starved vampire I admire the pulsating bursts of red liquid as I repeatedly slash. The walls and kitchen worktops are now coloured with it and yet I do not stop. Searching for more veins to open, I move towards my neck. I feel no pain as I cut horizontally from one side to the other. The blood runs down the middle, resembling a ruby necklace.

This is not enough. I search high and low for something to use as a tourniquet, and sneak off to the bathroom to continue. It is now half past two in the morning and everyone in the house is sleeping. I must remain quiet or they will discover what I have done. This is my time, my pleasure, and I do not want to be disturbed.

In a drawer I find large sewing needle. I slide it under the vein in my wrist to make it more accessible to my blade. Dissecting the vein, I feel a surge of sweet relief. I don't need medics to puncture my veins. I am indestructible. They may have inflicted this trauma on my baby boy, but I can do the same for myself. I am in control once more. As the viscous red blood pumps out, waves of suppressed emotion are released. The more blood I lose tonight, the easier the following day will be to deal with.

Now, I must cleanse and bandage my wounds. I need pain relief, so I swallow around 60 paracetamol, unaware of their immediate or long-term consequences.

Needing to engage a little piece of sanity from somewhere, anywhere, I call the Samaritans. They are engaged. The strength I had mustered to speak to someone dissipates.

I sit on the outside stairs. I have finished cutting myself for the time being, and I quietly contemplate my sorrow. It has been pouring now for over an hour, the rain pounding my body. By the security light in the back garden I can see a little river running down the garden path with streaks of my blood flowing through it. It is beautiful and somehow calming, as if it is washing all my pain away. Though my teeth are chattering and I am soaked and shivering, I feel nothing except for the crushing ache in my heart.

Why did I do such a horrid thing to myself? What have I achieved?

I have no answers: the last few hours have been worthless.

My husband's voice breaks into my thoughts. I jump with fright.

"What on earth have you done?" he shouts.

He rushes to me, takes my hands to pull me to my feet and ushers me inside the house out of the rain and the cold. He helps me change from my sodden nightclothes, then lays me down on top of my bed.

Shortly after, the paramedics arrive. They push on my shoulders and smack my face, trying to bring me round from drug-induced semi-consciousness. The doors to the house are all open and the cold air rushes in, and although I can smell the winter frost, I feel warm and drowsy in my bed. I don't want their attention.

"Please leave me alone," I say, "I am tired and I want to sleep."

But the paramedics are unsympathetic.

"No sympathy for self-inflicted harm," the female says

nastily to my husband.

He quickly comes to my defence: "I would rather you did not refer to my wife in this manner, and please don't handle her so roughly. You do not know what has brought her to this point."

The hefty woman hauls me from my cosy bed and pushes me firmly down onto a small metal chair. She wraps a blanket around me roughly, and straps me tightly in place. Her male colleague pushes me out to the waiting ambulance, and helps me inside. Gently, he rewraps the blanket around me after fastening the seat belt. I am so thankful the female paramedic is driving, and it is the male who is caring for me in the back.

The male asks me a hundred and one questions. I am trying very heard to stay conscious enough to answer him. He removes the bandages I had applied and uses stinging alcohol swabs to clean my wounds, then re-dresses them with sterile bandages.

"You seem to have a very caring husband," he says. "We have been to pick up people where there is no one who cares for them. It must be frightening for your husband to see you like this."

It has been two years since Stephen's diagnosis and many things have brought me to this state. I withhold the truth and reply that I don't know why I did something so silly.

The officer leaves me in casualty with kind words:
"You will get proper help in the hospital. They will
organise a psychologist to come and see you. I hope it
all works out for you."

As I lie in emergency a nurse comes to take my blood
pressure and temperature, and inquires as to how
many tablets I took and when I took them.

I ask for her understanding. "Please don't judge me," I
say, "I am not a bad person. It is just that sometimes I
can't cope with it all."

In my experience, there are not very many
compassionate nurses in the profession, but I was
lucky to have one at this time.

She says, "I am not here to judge anyone, you are here
because you are ill, and having an illness of the mind
is as real as a physically painful one. You will be OK
here. If you want to call anyone, or if there is anything
else you want, please let me know."

I am deeply grateful for her humanity.

Next thing, a drip is put in my arm so that I can
receive a medication to counteract the paracetamol I
have taken. I had been a regular blood donor, so
needles never bothered me. At the same time, the

nurses take a blood sample to check the amount of medication I will need. I am now left alone to wait four hours, after which they will take another blood sample to determine the dosage of the next round of medication.

Four hours on this hard table is a lifetime to wait. I am getting restless and irritated. I consider the needle in my arm. The little white plastic screw at the base of the cannula looks inviting. It seems to call me to open it, so I do.

The first gush of blood excites me. It is warm, and I can almost taste the iron, but I close it quickly in case a nurse spots me. I look around: the department seems to be quite quiet and I lust for another go. Opening the screw again, I feel powerful and defiant. This is my body, my blood, and I will do with it as I please. I decide to hide my arm under the sheet and leave the screw open – not fully, as that would bring a nurse too soon, but just enough to create a pool of redness. I feel that I have regained control of the situation, when so many times in the past I have been unable to influence events. Now it is my turn.

"Bloody hell, what is going on?" a nurse yells as she discovers the bloody puddle now forming on the floor.

Three of her colleagues run to my bedside. This is not what I wanted.

"What happened to your arm, did you do this?" the nurse demands.

I lie in silence; I will not explain myself to them.

I am pushed to another cubicle. The nurse calls the cleaning department, and since I am now in earshot of the nurses' station, I can listen to what they say about me.

"Stupid bitch, who does she think she is, does she think we have nothing better to do than clean up after her?"

I laugh inside – they don't know me or what I have been through.

The senior nurse now approaches. She asks me if I know how the tap in my arm became loose, but I remain silent once more.

Soon I am taken to a ward upstairs. I am aware that the staff in A&E have called beforehand to explain my details, and I know they told the ward staff to monitor my suicidal tendencies. On hearing this I decide to be the perfect patient, and once again regain control of the situation.

18

On reflection, the first few months after Stephen's first discharge from hospital were very strange. We were all on a great learning curve. Dr Donaldson's warning that balancing the amount of medication Stephen required for his diabetes insipidus would be difficult was a considerable understatement, I very quickly found out. However, as the time slowly moved on, we managed to read the signs from Stephen's behaviour and energy levels, and controlled the dosage that way.

Stephen's medications for his DI had to be kept cool at all times. As I was planning a short trip away, I needed a cool box. I contacted the Diabetic Association not realising that DI was quite different to the more common diabetes. They told me that they did not cover DI, but gave me the phone number of a charity that did know about DI – The Pituitary Foundation.

Dr Donaldson had given me a booklet about pituitary

conditions that affected Stephen, but I could hardly pronounce the complicated medical terminology. Nevertheless, armed with this literature I called the Foundation. A pleasant voice answered.

"Hello, the Pituitary Foundation, this is Sue, how can I help you?"

I said, "Hello, my son has a brain tumour called craniopharyngioma."

"Yes," she said.

"And diabetes insipidus."

"Yes."

"I don't know what else to tell you", I continued.

"That's OK, I know what you are talking about."

"Thank you very much, goodbye," I managed to stammer before hanging up the telephone.

I sat there speechless for an hour or so. I was incredulous that someone knew all about these horrible conditions. I felt utterly energised on hearing this – I had finally found people I could talk to, people who understood.

I called Sue again an hour or so later.

"I'm sorry I didn't explain myself before but you took my breath away because you knew what I was talking about."

"Don't worry about that", she replied. "It is usual for people to be quite shocked when they finally get to speak to someone with knowledge of these conditions. They are very frightening, and it comes as a great relief to people when they find us. How can I help?"

Finally, I was able to have a detailed conversation with an informed layperson about medication and the effects Stephen's condition was having on the family. Sue also gave me the name and number of the area coordinator for the Edinburgh support group, specialist endocrine nurse Maggie Carson.

When I asked Maggie if there was a support group closer to me she said, "No, but maybe in time we could have one if someone volunteers."

By the following year, guess who had volunteered to launch a support group in Glasgow?

I have never looked back since that first call to Sue Thorn at The Pituitary Foundation. Now we, The Glasgow Support Group, have a database of over 250 members. Many of these members have become friends and we get up to all sorts of wonderful fundraising events, as well as sharing the trauma and

19

It has been 18 months since my husband left, towards the end of 1998. I am now trying to overcome the hurt of this and rebuild a broken marriage, but it is made even more difficult with a very sick child.

"You're nobody till somebody loves you," says a song I heard as a child in the 70s. "You're nobody till somebody cares."

Who will care for me?

My husband had once said to me, as our child lay between us, "We will care for and love this child no matter what happens."

The next day, his thoughts had changed. "Let me go, I have found someone else and I don't want to be with you any more," he said.

I think back to the time when we were two people very much in love, and for so long. We have since become strangers. All the memories, all the promises and vows that were made, all the dreams we shared, are now broken.

Will there ever be a clear path back through all this?

Through all the enormous stress, we said and did many harsh things to each other, and at times there seems to be little hope of reconciliation. In any case, taking care of my personal difficulties and financially supporting my children is now uppermost in my mind.

As the months went by after his decision to split with me, my husband began to try desperately to treat me well and to help me with the care of Stephen. At first I refused any help from him as I was still too hurt, but my parents, concerned about my health, encouraged me to accept his assistance.

"After all," my father had said, "they are also his children; why should he not help with their care?"

Slowly – and I mean very slowly – we started to talk to each other in a more civil manner. I began to feel the pressure ease slightly when I knew my husband was coming to take the children out for the day and I could relax. On his return he would say how much he admired my strength, dealing with all Stephen's difficulties and still retaining a sense of humour. I knocked back his compliments, as I was reluctant to accept anything from him, even kind words.

Eventually, my husband made a major admission – that our marriage problems had been all his own doing. He said he couldn't and wouldn't ever forgive himself for being so selfish, hurting the woman he cherished so much and failing to support his young family when his son was so ill. He repeatedly explained that his fear of losing Stephen, and the prospect of having to arrange a funeral for his baby, was at the heart of his poor attendance at the hospital.

I thought less of him for that. We all have these thoughts, but they are no excuse to abandon a sick child, especially your own.

He would ask me daily, "How can I ever make up for all the hurt I have caused?"

But, on top of this struggle to negotiate a new relationship after all that had happened, we had a bigger problem: Stephen's eating.

20

Lying and cheating was not part of my children's behavioural repertoire before now, but Stephen was becoming an expert. He would steal food from anywhere. His propensity to eat himself to death loomed large over all our lives.

I dreaded our weekly visits to the supermarket. A typical shopping trip would go something like this: The shop is large, bright and busy. Stephen and I are wheeling around an overflowing trolley. I am tossing up in my mind what delights to conjure up for our evening meal. Nothing seems odd until I realise Stephen is missing.

Alarm sets in quickly.

Is he with store security and safe? Has he left the store with a stranger and is he now in danger? Has he had an accident, and if so do they know that I am in the store?

No, he has just succumbed once again to his eating disorder, hyperphagia, a consequence of hypothalamic damage sustained when his craniopharyngioma was removed. I know where to find him. With a deep-throated roar that would frighten any wild animal, I turn on my heels and head for the confectionery aisle. Stephen is there, sitting cross-legged on the floor with a mountain of sweet wrappers scattered around him. He has already eaten his way through most of the selection, but he insists it was not him who gobbled all the sweets.

This will be the third time this month.

Will the torment of this eating hell ever end?

It is not long before the security team arrives and escorts us both to the manager's office. I now must explain to the put-out management and the police why Stephen has done this, again, something I have had to do frequently between 1998 and 2004.

In addition, Stephen himself has had to come to terms with this aspect of his pituitary disorder, and learn to manage it. In answer to his questions – "What is wrong with me mum, and why am I still hungry after eating all of my meals, especially the vegetables?" – I have to try to explain a very difficult medical condition to a little boy:

"Your tummy and your head have fallen out with each other," I repeat time and again, "and do not speak to each other anymore. So you are going to have to be brave and strong and help them. Your tummy does not remember when you ate anything, and your head will keep telling your tummy to eat more. You will have to be the in-between person and speak to both of them. When your head tells you you are hungry, you must remember that this is not true."

I wonder if he understands what I am trying so hard to explain.

For Stephen, managing his hunger is an enormous task, especially as his only thought, day-by-day, hour-by-hour, minute-by-minute, is where to get his next food fix. He will seek any kind of food, at any cost; he will rake through cupboards and even eat scraps from dinner tables if they are within reach. He will steal and has stolen food from lunch boxes, bags, and trolleys – from anywhere – to try to satisfy his insatiable appetite. At breakfast he would ask what was for lunch, at lunch he would ask what was for dinner, and so it goes on.

The most effective method I found to regulate Stephen's hyperphagia was to have meals at the same time every day. I taught Stephen how to tell the time, which helps a lot but does not stop him wanting more. We put a large poster on the kitchen wall, with all our meal times and menus for the day. After each meal, it was Stephen's job to write down what he had eaten and if he had enjoyed it. His account was very detailed. He noted down each portion size, and the number of vegetables, whether they be potatoes, sprouts, or even peas. This was intended to remind him of what and when he had consumed. Still, at some point each day he would call us all liars and insist he had not eaten, even when we had all had our meals together.

This chronic conflict alone was putting a great strain on our household. As well, Sam and Kirsty were getting fed up with being denied treats. In time, this problem caused the rest of us to overeat when Stephen was in hospital as he frequently was, or when he was at school, causing me especially to gain an enormous amount of weight.

In fact, it is hard to convey the effects this seemingly innocuous disorder has had on our family. For one thing, it has been soul destroying to watch Stephen struggle with his condition, and I cannot even imagine what it feels like from his point of view.

There have been times when my seven year old son has been so angry that he has gotten hold of a knife and cut his wrists, wanting to die to end his torment. He has put the gas cooker on during the night and burned wooden spoons out of the sheer frustration of his unsatisfied hunger. He has taken a rock and scratched the length of our car, and broken windows.

On many occasions he has run out the house, far down the street, irrespective of the time of day or the weather or what he was wearing (sometimes just underpants).

I have had many fierce battles with my son, and sustained hundreds of bruises, bites, scratches and punches along the way. I have sat on my bed and cried myself to sleep on many nights, wondering, dreading, what the next day's horrors would be. It is especially difficult because I know Stephen cannot help himself.

Eventually I vented this frustration on myself.

At a deeper level, I worry about what will happen when Stephen is an adult. Who will look after his eating plan then? People will be less tolerant and caring when he is grown, and I anticipate him getting into trouble with the police and authorities. I hope we can find help for him before this happens.

Some of the nursing staff at the hospital and teachers at his school have also come under fire, but to my relief he has never hurt another child. I suppose this is because the other children do not have anything to do with his food intake. However, another aspect of his condition that affects his socialisation is inappropriate and inept social behaviour, including temper tantrums. These are especially challenging because of the difficulty of controlling an obese and powerful child.

Still other barriers compound Stephen's problems. He has become lonely and isolated from his peer group as they all have much more energy than he has, and the other kids have a terrific time playing games with him, tricking, bullying and teasing him about sweets.

We have had a major problem trying to find a school that could deal with such problems, because children with disorders like Stephen's rarely have learning disabilities. On the contrary, they can be more intelligent than their peers, and therefore most of the traditional special schools for disabled children are not suitable.

Our social worker and her team have attempted on many occasions to convince the authorities that Stephen needs a particular type of education. We have had many group meetings with an array or medical and educational professionals: the specialist endocrine nurse, psychiatrist, psychologist, school paediatrician, social worker, head teacher, class teacher, local educational psychologist and the educational psychologist from the neighbouring district.

The only appropriate school is in another area, but this district must give priority to its local children's needs. We had to arrange for Stephen's consultant and our GP to write letters to assist in our application. Ultimately we were put at the end of a long waiting list and, to our delight, after all the local children were placed in the school there was a place left for Stephen. He is now in his first year of secondary school and has settled in very well.

The school has a great schedule for him to which he has been very responsive. He even works at the tuck shop – supervised of course – and all the other kids love him. Finally, we are now a little less concerned about his days at school.

For the time being, at least, I need not worry too much about his education.

21

As days go by in April 2000, Stephen begins to feel unwell, but it hard to put a finger on what is wrong. I telephone the specialist nurse, who advises that I bring him into hospital for the doctors to check him over. Stephen undergoes the usual routine of bloods and questions, but the medicos do not seem to think anything serious is going on. They provisionally diagnose a viral infection.

I am not at all satisfied and refuse to leave until they do a CT scan for confirmation.

I am quickly told that the CT scanner's daily schedule is full, and if I insist on Stephen having a scan today, I will need to wait until the end of the day. I explain that I have no problem waiting. My son's health is far more important than a few uncomfortable hours for me, and it is most important for my peace of mind to rule out any further problems. We wait about five hours for a gap in the schedule.

To my distress, when the young student doctor comes back with the results, she sits on Stephen's bed and begins a discussion she should not have.

Looking at Stephen, she speaks bluntly and with no preamble: "The CT scan has shown us that your tumour is back, and it is as big as the first time."

The look of on Stephen's little face and his cries of fear were almost too much to bear.

"No mummy, please, I don't want to have another operation on my head!"

What kind of training has this junior doctor had if she thinks it is acceptable to speak like this in front of a sick child?

I look directly at the doctor and express my displeasure in no uncertain terms. "I don't think this is the right place to have this conversation, do you think we could go outside."

All at once, I am hurled back into the nightmare I thought I had left permanently behind.

The specialist nurse comes to see us at the end of her shift around 5.30pm, and tries to put me at ease.

She says, "I didn't think anything was wrong with Stephen, except maybe a virus or something trivial. I am glad you stuck to your guns and waited for a scan today."

It is little consolation. The thought of what may have happened to Stephen if I had not waited churns my stomach. I am left asking the same old questions.

Why do the medical people not believe me when I say Stephen is ill? I would have thought by now they would take my opinion more seriously.

I am instructed to take Stephen home tonight, but go to the neurosurgery hospital first thing in the morning. The endocrine nurse has already called them, and they know of our imminent arrival.

The news the next day is not good. Stephen must immediately have more surgery to drain a cyst that is over his re-grown tumour. The neurosurgeon explains that the tumour is again very large. The plan is to try to remove what can safely be excised, and, most importantly, to get Stephen started on a course of radiotherapy.

The anaesthetist visits us and explains the procedure they will undertake tomorrow morning to avoid the problems Stephen had last time with his veins. He assures Stephen and myself that things will be a lot easier this time round. This does not help much where

Stephen is concerned, but I spend many hours reassuring him.

At 8am the anaesthetist returns to Stephen's bed and gives him a little drink of pre-med to make him slightly drowsy and reduce his anxiety. They decide to try to put the drips into Stephen while he is still in the ward, as this will be less frightening than in the pre-theatre room.

It all goes to plan.

The outcome of the surgery, however, was not so positive. Directly afterwards the surgeon informs us that, having seen the re-growth, she does not intend to go back to surgery in the future. All our hopes now hang on radiotherapy.

I feel bereft.

What will happen to Stephen if the radiotherapy does not work?

22

We are now in a new department.

As we look around, we see that all the other patients here have lost their hair as a side effect of their treatment.

"Will I lose all of my hair mummy?" Stephen asks.

I explain to him that these people have a different illness from his, and he won't lose all his hair.

With sadness in his sweet eyes he says, "But I wanted to lose my hair and be like my daddy."

I am amazed, again, at my little boy's courage, and his unique perspective on life. Everyone else is making such a big fuss of hair loss, and Stephen is more upset that he won't be going bald.

The Beatson oncology department does not treat

many children and the effort they all put into cheering Stephen up was phenomenal. This is our second visit and today they must make a mask of Stephen's face before the treatment can commence. Plaster of Paris will be put all over his little face with only a straw in his mouth to breathe through. I am worried about how Stephen will cope.

Will I need to hold my baby down again?

The thought haunts me. Luckily, if that is what you could call it, the nursing staff are so tender in explaining the process to Stephen as they perform it, stopping anytime he asks, and reassuring him when the difficult bit is almost over, that he manages to tolerate it. I on the other hand am deeply unsettled at the sight of my baby's face completely covered with the hardening, tightening plaster.

"Only another few minutes," the nurse says to Stephen.

I don't know if Stephen wants to say anything in reply, but he cannot.

This time my husband is at my side. We have continued to try to come to terms with all that has passed between us, but we both know we have a rocky path to conquer. At least I know Stephen is more contented this time, having both his parents with him.

As we commence the radiotherapy, we live in hope. It had better work, as it is our only weapon against the quick and unexpected return of the tumour.

Stephen will receive 25 consecutive days of treatment every morning at 9am, followed by meetings with his consultants to review the risks.

The first two days of treatment go well and the fondness of the nurses for their child patients, including Stephen, makes it bearable. The actual treatment only takes about two to five seconds, but the radiation will go on working for many years.

As we depart, the radiotherapist advises us of the side effects of treatment and the precautions we need to take: "You have to wear a hat, Stephen, or the sunshine will burn the two balding sides of your head."

With his hair gone there is no protection, and the skin there is very thin. Grumpily, my little boy puts on his hat, but with a face that would break your heart.

"I wanted to show everyone my balding bits mum," he mumbles.

We were also told that the major side effects including nausea and vomiting would begin towards the end of his 25 treatments. This was not to be – Stephen begins to suffer from the start. Here comes of another difficult day, I think to myself, as gray cardboard sick bowls and empty tissue boxes fill the back seat of the car on our way home.

Why does my son have to go on suffering?

Things change for the worse again by day three. When we arrive home after Stephen's treatment, he starts to vomit. This continues through the night, and he becomes dehydrated. We try to talk him into sipping water but every time he does he vomits again. I know it is time to call his specialist nurse, as dehydration in DI patients can be perilous, and Stephen's needs treatment.

"Bring him to the hospital immediately," says the nurse when I call her. "Do you have transport or will I send an ambulance?"

Stephen is admitted to hospital for the remainder of the radiotherapy treatment.

As the days of his treatment go by, Stephen becomes more dehydrated, despite the drip giving him vital fluids and the anti-nausea medication. Yet the course of 25 radiation treatments must be finished if he is to have a chance to fight this tumour.

Stephen's lack of energy means he spends long periods motionless on the bed, and the sound of a slight cough alerts us to a new problem. The physiotherapist confirms that, as Stephen is immobile, he runs the risk of developing life-threatening pneumonia. The physiotherapy team works around the clock in shifts to give Stephen gentle exercises to help his lungs expand, and they manage to acquire a special mattress to take some pressure off his little bones.

With Stephen in hospital I divide up my days to fit in as much as possible. It is an especially busy time: after waiting to relocate for two years since Stephen's diagnosis, we have now been offered a new house. I suddenly have two weeks to prepare the new house, pack up the old, and move.

Why now?

The new place needs an enormous amount of decorating done, and this is taking its toll. As always, however, I will work through this. At least now my husband is here to help with the move, even though the family has always had a little chuckle over his attempts at decorating.

23

I get to the hospital around 8.30am every day, join
Stephen and his medical support team to go the other
hospital where he has his treatment, go back to the
children's hospital for an hour or so, then head home.
After a light lunch I spend a couple of hours packing
boxes and emptying wardrobes and drawers, and then
I go to our new house.

My husband visits Stephen for a while on his way
home from work, then goes home, collects Sam, and
brings him to our new house where we all muck in
with some painting and cleaning.

Kirsty is on holiday with her grandparents in sunny
Spain. There are fewer of us to visit Stephen, pack up
the old house and get the new house ready, so the
stress is quickly building for the three of us.

Nearer bedtime we all go to visit Stephen again, then
return home and collapse.

This was to be our routine for the next four weeks of Stephen's treatment. But due to an unforeseen incident with the special mattress, things changed. By the end of the next week, this mattress was to cause more problems than it relieved.

By week three Stephen was not getting any better and Dr Donaldson considered putting a hold on the radiotherapy until he gained more strength. However, after extensive talks with Stephen's medical team, it was decided to proceed but watch him very closely for any major relapse.

The nursing staff by now knew our family very well and would wheel a telephone to the side of Stephen's bed and help him make an occasional call home. The nurses knew we were moving house at this time and that my visits were not as long as I would have wanted.

On one call I was shocked to hear Stephen crying and begging me to come and take him home. I told him he would be OK, and that I would see him in the morning.

Stephen protested, though he so lacked strength that he could raise barely a whisper. "My back hurts, mummy, and the nurses woke me up to take the soft mattress away and they won't come and rub my back."

I called the ward and asked to speak to the nurse taking care of Stephen. She was on her lunch break, so I left a message for her to call me. After waiting over an hour, I called her back. Her reply to my query about the removal of the bed was very vague. She said she knew nothing about it, but would find out and get back to me.

Again, I waited, but my patience was thinning, I only wanted to know why they had taken this mattress away. Dr Donaldson had put a lot of effort into accessing it for Stephen as he was critically ill. If he had authorised its removal I knew he would have had a good reason to do so. I only wanted the circumstances confirmed.

I had to call back a second time, and the answer I received threw me. A child had been admitted to another ward, and the parents had insisted that their child should have a softer mattress. I could not believe my ears – on the basis of these parents' demands my sick child had been woken and forced to surrender his only bit of comfort.

I was furious. I asked if the nursing staff had contacted Stephen's doctor to get his permission.

Apparently not. "Stephen is not the only patient we have and we cannot go around tending only to him," I was told.

With steam coming from my ears and tears coursing down my face I got into the car and drove straight to the hospital. I was still wearing my old smelly clothes as I had been painting our new house. I marched over to Stephen, dressed him, put him into his wheelchair and walked out.

By the time we got home there was a police car waiting.

Because I had taken Stephen from the hospital without signing a form, the nursing staff had called the police and the social work team. They had treated me like some sort of criminal. Yet it was their treatment of my defenceless son that had precipitated my actions.

After I got Stephen settled into my bed, the social worker began bombarding me with questions. She had also been given a list of all the medication Stephen took, and wanted to make sure I had all of these at home.

"Do you realise" she went on, "that if anything goes wrong with Stephen you cannot hold the hospital responsible?"

"What do I care," I replied. "The stupid nursing staff have been bullied by another child's parents and rather than face up to them, the nurses chicken out and make my sick child suffer. They can rot in hell for all I care."

Unsurprisingly, the social worker sprang to the defence of the nursing staff: "I don't think there is any need for that, and I am more worried about Stephen's health now that he is alone with you in this mental state."

Furious, but catching on to her insinuation, I decide to reply in a conciliatory fashion.

"I do appreciate all that the nursing staff do, but I was upset at Stephen crying about the removal of the mattress. If I think he is becoming more unwell I will contact the ward immediately."

On that note, the police and social worker decide to leave.

Later, Stephen asks me a question I have trouble answering: "How long will I be sick mum?"

"I don't know, son, but each time you are sick, you are letting out all the bad bits in your head, so the more times you are sick the better you will be."

I am running out of answers to his questions.

24

Thunder is booming outside, and although it is July the sky is dark and gray. The new house does not have any working heating yet, and as there are no carpets or window coverings it feels cold and somehow hollow.

Since I have been forced by circumstances to look after Stephen at home, he spends his days on a garden lounger in the empty front room. It is not an ideal set-up. The house smells damp, and every time we make sandwiches and a hot cup of tea we can taste the wallpaper paste no matter how many times I wash my hands and all the kitchen work surfaces.

I try to go on decorating around his sick times, which, as always, are heartbreaking. I would love to take Stephen to our old home, put him into my bed and nurse him there, where I know he would feel more secure, but I cannot. At times, when he gets really tired, I take the cushion off the sun lounger and put it on the floor. I take the extra quilt I have brought to the new house and cover him up, then lie beside him on the bare cold floor and remind him of happier times we have spent on holidays or at the park with his brother and sister. This helps him nod off, and on more than one occasion I have dropped off to sleep myself.

As I look at my sleeping son, I try to think of a way to cheer him up with very limited resources. I take all the old doorframes and skirting boards we have removed and build a bonfire in the back garden. I wait for Stephen to wake up and show him what I have done. We get the garden chairs and go outside to sit nearer the bonfire. At last we have some heat.

Although the new house has special adaptations for Stephen, we no longer have a loft space. Sadly, all the children's things and memorabilia have to be sorted through and scaled down.

25

"When all is calm, and you are home and settled, this is when depression sets in," the doctor said. "This is when you have time to consider all that has been happening. What we need to do is to catch the potential depression before is becomes a downward spiral."

Good advice, I thought, but it doesn't help assuage the still-present trauma or answer the questions that remain.

Why me? Why my son? Why my husband?

One of my old friends, a regular church attendee, once replied to one of these questions.

"God knew that when Stephen was being made he was going to have special needs and God wanted him to go to a special mother, so he decided to give Stephen to you."

This sentiment made me cry. It was the most beautiful thing anyone had said to me throughout my entire ordeal, and it helped me through many difficult times.

Hour and hours of speaking to my psychologist brings me to a different perspective on my thoughts and feelings, too. Visiting her is my last attempt at getting help.

The beautiful Victorian building which houses her clinic is set back within a wall of trees just off the main road. The architecture is unique, and as it is now mid November there is a light flurry of snow lying on the ground. Walking up the path the scrunch of the gravel recalls the sound of horses' hooves in earlier times. With the old gas lamp posts still in place, it is possible to imagine the house at the centre of a gently lit winter scene on an antiquated Christmas card.

As each session began with the therapist, I would typically say, "I have nothing to talk about today."

For her part, she might on occasion provocatively ask, "How many plates do you think you can spin before they all come tumbling down?"

Then, while she sat in unhurried silence, things would begin to come from nowhere. Before long, I was in full swing. Consistently, I would return to my preoccupation with my feelings for my husband, and the damage done in our split.

In one session, I recounted the moment it all started. We were organising a charity disco on a Saturday morning. As my husband prepared the music, I was suffocating in the hot kitchen preparing food. When we took a break, I noticed that my husband looked out of sorts.

"Why the long face?" I asked.

His answer blew me off my feet.

"I am going to leave."

"Leave what?"

"All of this, you, the kids."

"Why?" I asked, at once bewildered and gutted.

His reply was hurtful and confusing. "I think I have met someone else and I might go and stay with her. I am not sure yet but I will let you know in nine days. I don't want to run our business anymore – you can do what you want with it."

I sat in silence for a few minutes until the enormity of his words sank in. Finally, I made my way across the room. I kneeled at his feet and looked tenderly up at him.

"What is wrong? I can fix it what ever it is."

By the look on his face I knew this was serious. I began to beg.

"Please Stephen, please don't leave me, please. I will do what ever it takes to make you stay. Please don't bring on me the shame of my husband leaving."

He was not interested in my pleas.

"Get up! Do you know how stupid you look? I am thinking of leaving and I may be going to stay with someone else – that is all you need to know. I will tell you more in nine days."

As I stood up, young Stephen came into the room and asked why I was crying. I lied and said I didn't feel very well.

That evening we went through with the charity disco, raising a lot of money for a worthy cause. But I left alone with my kids and my husband stayed out all night. Where he was I don't know.

As the days went by I confided in my friends about what has transpired between my husband and myself.

One friend, Violet, said to me, "Tell me all that again –

the whole story."

Once I had finished, she explained who she thought this other person was.

I was astonished at her speculation on the identity of the other woman. I always thought men left their wives and children for young beautiful woman, not middle aged, ugly ones with children of their own.

I went straight home and called the husband of my rival. His first words shocked me.

"Is your husband the one who works in the pub called the Tavern?"

"Yes," I said. My fears were tacitly confirmed. Then, all of a sudden, I felt the sharp pain of breathlessness, just as I had when I thought I would lose Stephen.

I gathered up my children, drove to my mother-in-law's house where my husband was staying, and confronted him with this information.

He couldn't care less. "So what!" he said dismissively. "Leave me alone, I am tired and I want to sleep."

Around this time my son's headaches were getting worse. I was affording him less attention than I should, as I was going through my own acute trauma. Now that I know what he was suffering, I am wracked with guilt.

I recall also, that during this time we had gone to our daughter's school to see a show in which she was participating. My husband chose this moment to make a bizarrely inappropriate confession. "I feel as though I have met my soul mate," he said.

How could he sit by my side at our daughter's debut and tell me he had found his soul mate in someone else? Is this man totally heartless or just plain stupid?

I was flabbergasted. I thought of all the time we had loved each other.

Were all the years of happy marriage false and empty for him?

As the weeks turned into months I was becoming stronger emotionally, and thinner physically, as I had not much of an appetite. All of a sudden he was paying me more interest than he had for some years.

But having made his announcement that he wished to leave, every day after work he would come to my house and sit crying, asking me to help him with his decision. It was beyond belief.

I am the one he has abandoned and he is asking me to help him with his problems? What a nerve. Who will help me?

All the while, true to form I tormented myself with unanswerable questions about his reasons for deserting us.

What did I do that is so wrong to make my husband leave?

Desperate for answers and feeling unworthy of anyone's love, I turned to drinking alcohol and self harm.

During this period, my dad, a very proud and faithful man of few words, offered me some sound advice: "Soldier on love, soldier on," he said.

These were words I took to heart. And in the end, I followed his advice.

I worked fulltime, cared for our three kids and kept the house in good order. My husband, on the other hand, was being used as a sitter for someone else's young children while she went about her business ruining another marriage.

I now remembered a conversation I had had with this tramp some time ago. She told me she had been repeatedly raped by her father and his friends, and that she was contemptuous of men and set on ruining every man's life that she could.

Eventually my sucker of a husband, who had been led to believe he was the best thing since sliced bread, realised he had been used.

At that stage, it was too late. He had taken too great a liberty with my good nature, and as far as I was concerned, his time as husband and father was over. Nor were our young children impressed with their father's actions.

As for me, I tried to be brave in front of everyone, especially my children and my parents. But my heart had been broken, and was unlikely, I thought then, ever to be repaired.

Epilogue

I haven't been drinking or self-harming for two months now. Although this is significant progress, I am not getting my hopes up too high. My psychologist says there is always a chance of a relapse. I am just taking things day-by-day.

I am still trying to come to terms with what has happened in my life over the past few years. But now, instead of trying to apportion blame, I see that there are lessons to be learnt.

Whereas I used to be so fragile, now I have good days – days where I can see and feel a difference. There is an undercurrent driving me in a positive, expansive direction.

My husband and I are slowly making our way back towards one another, to a new found and deeper understanding of love, but most of all, to a new sense of mutual respect.

I know he worries desperately about me. I see anxiety in his face now. He is always watching out for telltale signs of re-emerging problems.

Is she upset? Who upset her? Is there any alcohol she could get a hold of?

He is once again there for me.

Not so long ago I almost lost my child and my husband, and they almost lost me. What I did lose, eventually, was my loving parents. Their passing, although sudden and terribly painful, brought home the reality and beauty of life to me.

Stephen has had a few rough patches since the beginning of his trauma at the tender age of seven years.

He is now 13 years old – at the start of his teenage years – and aware of the difficult and painful condition he has to live with. He manages to inject himself daily with his medication, and take the pills he must to keep alive.

What delights or trauma will his years of adolescence bring?

We, his family, now have become quite expert with his medication and mood swings. We are able to defuse many potentially difficult situations before they become troublesome.

Stephen is doing very well in school. He has reached the government standards in his education, which is quite remarkable as he lost almost three years of his early schooling.

It is Christmastime again, and we are all rugged up in winter woollies. We are off to the Glasgow town centre to enjoy the beauty of the festive lights and nativity scene.

This time things will be different. Together as a family, we are ready for the happy and peaceful times that lie ahead.

A letter from Pat McBride, a lady who has now become a very close and special family friend through shared experience of a pituitary disorder.

An adult patient's view of children with pituitary disease

On Friday February 11 2000 I stepped off a train at Glasgow Station, and was greeted warmly by Irene Coombe and her son Stephen, the first child with pituitary disease I had seen or met.

I've had pituitary disease for 17 years, and coincidentally suffer from most of the problems that Stephen has. We have hypopituitarism, meaning basically that our pituitary glands don't function, and we have to take replacement hormones. We've both endured craniotomies – brain surgery – and Stephen has had two of these operations, plus radiotherapy.

With our comparable conditions in mind, I envisaged a young boy who would have similar daily quests and minor problems to those I had. These are challenges that I had come to accept readily due to the improvements in my health brought about by hormone replacements, and the sheer necessity of 'getting on with it'. I looked forward to our meeting as the train sped on through increasingly frost-covered fields towards Scotland.

I remember Stephen's lovely twinkly smile, and a great big hug which made me fill up inside. I may be wrong, but he seemed to be saying in that hug, "here is someone who will understand." This eight year old boy had just turned my thoughts on the train upside down – I didn't have the knowledge or experience with pituitary children to begin to conceive of just how dreadfully cruel to little ones this disease could be. I had met many adult patients with varying degrees of the disease, and knew that the majority of these people had found a coping mechanism, if not come to accept it.

Stephen slowly hobbled – the only word I can use – towards the car, across the station car park. His joints ached under the pressure of a body bloated by steroids and his inability to control his appetite, a stark fact of hypothalamic damage. He had great difficulty in manoeuvring himself onto the rear seat, and hurt himself as he tried. He cried tears of pain and frustration – once again I was choked. I wished that I could take away this horror from him.

I spent the next two days with Stephen and his family. I also met other children with pituitary disease, particularly with craniopharyngioma, the tumour Stephen suffered, and there were many similarities amongst these young people.

As for me, I simply take hormones to control my

condition: I have tablets three times a day, snort vasopressin via a nostril to control DI (diabetes insipidus), plus I have self-administered injections each night. No big deal. It was a positive experience to actually take my hormones around the same time of day as Stephen, so that we could be the 'same'. But as I joined him in his medication rituals, I began to see the sheer hard work, and sometimes dread, of a mother trying to get an eight year old to swallow/inject chemicals – often awful tasting if not swallowed fast – on a daily basis over a number of years. Combined with this, Stephen was having nightmares, had difficulties with thirst/fluid control and was vomiting regularly. So, up came the last dose of essential cortisol – how much had he digested?

He couldn't just say, "Bye mum, I'm off out to play." Firstly he didn't have the energy or the mobility, and his frustrating mood swings limited or often halted his relationships with other children. I, as an adult, also suffer mood swings due to my condition, albeit less intense than Stephen's, but I am able to modify my behaviour so as to fit in more with others. A child with this trauma must feel exasperated, and naturally doesn't have the maturity to understand or cope with these horrible hormonal flashes of altered mood.

I know that, in an ideal world, children should never suffer any disease or impairment, not only pituitary ones. My experience of being with Stephen taught me that pituitary disease, especially, should never touch children. In the pituitary world, blood tests, clinic appointments, claustrophobic MRI scans, and constant medication are the norm – for life.

Adults look upon this as a chore to be got through as quickly as possible, but what do the children think and go through?

I'm also humbled by how child patients continue their difficult daily life, and I can now really appreciate how their parents face each problem and work around or through it, motivating and supporting their sons and daughters. They have faced, and will continue to face, many more challenges than we adult patients will ever have.

My thanks to Stephen, who helped me to open my eyes more, and to understand what the word 'brave' truly means, and to his family, who are a true example of loving and caring in a nearly impossible situation.

Pat McBride
October 2003

Motherhood

"Children think that we are their strength,
but the truth is they are ours."

===========================

Book cover illustration
By
Pat McBride

C/O
The Pituitary Foundation
Po Box 1944
Bristol
BS99 2UB

www.pituitary.org.uk

Printed in the United States
by Baker & Taylor Publisher Services